A SPELL OF THR

MEMOIRS OF A CHILDHOOD IN CORNWALL

Penny Humphrey

Henscath House circa 1942

1

Thank you to the memory of my husband Ray

who

encouraged me for years to write my

memories of Cornwall

Thank you to my grown up children

Nicola Matthew and Victoria (T)

for their support and to

Paula Napier and Nicola for their patient help

in getting this published

This book is dedicated

to the memory of

my parents Betty and Q Killick

and my sister Wendy

Contents

CHAPTER ONE

Caught by the Spell
1942-1945

The beginning nearly didn't happen.
In September 1942, Betty and Q Killick
arrived in Cornwall to spend one night in
Penzance at the Star hotel in Market Jew
street, before journeying on to Mullion for
a short honeymoon. They wanted to spend
a few days away from the stress of living
and working in war torn London. The
proprietor welcomed them and they
deposited their bags in their room and
went in search of the bar for a night cap.
Planes were heard droning overhead,
German planes. The room went quiet and
heads turned upwards listening. The
planes were flying low and the sound of
the engines was deafening, within seconds
a dull heavy thud followed by a huge
explosion, the building shook and glasses
rattled and shattered as everyone in the
bar threw themselves to the floor and
under tables, breathlessly waiting and
praying that the building didn't fall in on
them but the Star hotel mercifully
remained standing. It was the building
next door that had been hit and by some
great providence not one person was killed
that night.

Cornwall was not the safe haven far away from London that it may have seemed in the second world war. The huge natural harbour of Falmouth took war ships for repair and Newlyn took big boats too. The naval airbase of Culdrose was in the extreme south west as well and so there were plenty of prime targets for German bombers.

Apparently, the bomb that fell that night was intended for the new telephone exchange that had just been built nearby on Market Jew Street but which was not touched by the bomb or its blast.

The next day shaken but undeterred, Betty and Q travelled the remaining twenty or so miles further down the peninsula where they were to spend a week in a small bed and breakfast bungalow called appropriately, Journey's End, along the cliffs at Mullion. The bungalow is still there much as it ever was but the cliff edge is eroding closer each year and has already claimed one house built on the opposite side of the lane.

Q, already under the spell of south west Cornwall, was keen to show Betty the magic of the place and they spent the week strolling the paths around them, walking over the cliffs to Kynance cove scattered around with its huge dark serpentine rocks glistening on the beach of yellow sand as if some enormous giant had randomly tipped stones out of his pockets.

The walk to Kynance across the cliffs from Mullion takes several hours at strolling pace and the steep undulating terrain can be quite taxing but worth every step because of its continually changing vistas and just sheer beauty. In the summer there are carpets of wild flowers and especially thrift or sea pinks which hug the steep grassy inclines that flow down over high cliff faces to the sea. Nearly half of the British Native flora can be found here as well as the common sea campion, vetch and trefoils. The colours are ever changing throughout the seasons from purple heather to the bright yellow gorse.

The last part of the walk down into Kynance cove from Mullion side, is steep and hazardous and in fact there is no easy and certainly no drivable way to it from either side. The cove is so compelling that the difficult access does not deter visitors who flocked there in their thousands every year and still do.

Nearby, the Lizard village, the most South westerly point of England has its own charm and singular identity, a moody place like the end of the earth at times. I remember grey mizzly days at the Lizard when it could look very drab and depressing but when the sun is shining it assumes a very different mantle, it is uplifting and full of optimism, little shops and cafes and pubs surround the large green in the centre where you can sit with fish and chips or a Cornish pasty. From here you can walk the steep cliff path down to Church cove past the much painted and photographed thatched cottages or go to visit the Lifeboat station down on the rocks and the Lizard lighthouse with its huge revolving light sitting in a bed of mercury warning boats away from the jagged coastline and the treacherous Manacles which have claimed many a boat from where they lie in wait just under the surface of the water.

In Lizard village in the forties and fifties there were many small workshops where serpentine both red and green were shaped into lighthouses, ashtrays and other ornaments, the serpentine when polished, having a wonderful sheen like lacquer. The items were sold in the shops and provided a good income for the workers. Outside one of the serpentine shops I remember there were glass cased mechanical scenes where for a penny in the slot you could watch a mechanical man doll working at his craft chiselling a piece of serpentine and working a foot propelled polishing machine. On reflection

my sister and I probably got as much
excitement from watching those
mechanical dolls as a child would now
from a trip to Legoland.

Times have changed and serpentine is
protected to some degree and that
particular cottage industry is now much
depleted although there are still
serpentine objects to be bought at the
Lizard which are made under licence.

A little further east along the cliffs below
the village of Ruan Minor is the tiny
Cadgwith cove, approached from either
side by an extremely steep single track
road. There are car parks these days
above the cove so you can walk the pretty
track to the village. Cadgwith has a magic
all of its own, the houses scattered like
sprinkles on a cake, are mostly white
washed and thatched, the old granite
pilchard cellars remain and the lifeboat
house which was still in use into the
Sixties provides memories of the many
lives lost at sea. The now redundant
lifeboat station is used by the Cadgwith
pilot gig club. A stream meanders down
the valley through the lush vegetation
provided by its sheltered micro climate. It
spills out onto the stony beach where
fishing boats have been pulled up over the
centuries. The Cadgwith cove pub has
been the focus of village social life there

for many years and in the bar on a Friday night around ten o'clock the Cadgwith singers begin their renditions of traditional Cornish folk songs. The fishermen sing with such spirit that you cannot fail to be moved and their voices boom out across and into the water where many of their fishing friends have been lost to the clutches of the sea.

Q and Betty visited as many places as they could in the short space of time they had there, the coves such as Coverack, Cadgwith, Poltesco and those around Mullion village, Poldhu, Polurrian and Gunwalloe with its tiny church of St Wynwalloe on the North side of the beach, with its separate tower built into the hard rock of the headland. They visited the City of Truro with its magnificent cathedral and they saw the pretty towns of Falmouth and Helston. By the end of their whirl wind visit there Betty had caught the magic of South West Cornwall too.

They had met while Q was a manager at La Porte Industries, in Bedfordshire, which much later was to become Fullers Earth. I remember my father telling my sister Wendy and me that he had been standing on an internal bridged passageway between two of the office buildings at La Porte, talking to a colleague, when my mother a new employee, was walking

underneath them. He looked down and watched her for a few moments and said to his colleague. "I'm going to marry that girl" and true to his word he did.
After their honeymoon they would be moving into London for a while where Q had taken a senior position in the Civil Defence, dangerous work in the centre of the City, visiting and assessing newly bombed areas and giving lectures to new recruits. He must have seen some harrowing sights but rarely spoke of them. Although he did later tell of the night he was called to assess the immediate danger of a massive bomb crater in the middle of a street. Smoke was rising out of the debris and there was a distinct smell of town gas enveloping the air around them. The town gas, so much more toxic than the natural gas used now, would have to be addressed straight away. Q stood on the edge of the crater with a colleague whilst they decided how big an area of people must be evacuated immediately. The local population was moved out to halls and churches at a safe distance. Within a very short time of the evacuation there was a massive explosion, not only had the bomb hit a gas main but unbeknown to anyone, there was another larger undetonated bomb which now exploded with terrifying force and noise

bringing down buildings nearby. Only ten minutes before, Q had returned and stood again at the edge deciding whether the situation needed reassessing, whilst waiting for the gas experts. He only moved away from the scene because he happened to be called to another situation.

Betty spent much of the war years driving ambulances across London, dangerous and emotionally draining work. One night she had gone to pick up a man with a suspected broken back. She had to drive him at five miles an hour across London to a hospital in order to achieve as smooth a ride as possible for the patient and not jolt him. Half way across the city the air raid sirens went off but there was nothing for it but to continue slowly with her fragile load and now without the help of headlights. Thankfully she made it to the hospital.

Q and Betty were a popular and handsome couple and any time off was spent at dances and driving to the country on saved petrol coupons. My father tall and debonair, my mother had a striking resemblance to Vivien Leigh the actress and was asked for her autograph on several occasions.

The contrast between their arduous jobs in London and the serenity of the South West Cornish coast line must have been very great.

Q was restless, he had a passion for Cornwall and before the war, he visited the Lizard area many times with his friends Ron and Eric, walking the coastal paths and visiting the glorious coves and bays, exploring the challenging primeval moors and the fairy land valleys running down to the sea.

They walked up to the Old Inn in the village on that first evening in Mullion and were welcomed by the proprietors, David and Joan Truscott, their first meeting with a couple who would become their lifelong friends.

It was towards the end of their stay in Mullion that Q admitted to Betty that what had started a few years before as a whim, had become an obsession. He wanted to live in Cornwall, preferably in this extreme South West corner. He didn't want to wait for retirement but rather just until the end of the war whenever that might be. He knew it was a very big ask, Betty having spent her life in London was very much a city girl and so it must have been with some trepidation that she found herself agreeing to my father's mad-cap idea of giving up a very comfortable life at the other end of the country and taking a house in Porthleven or Mullion but if she was later to regret it, she never said so.

They went to the Old Inn to mull it over with David and Joan who were delighted with the idea and David told them of a house currently taken over by the Government for RAF personnel who were operating from their station on Goonhilly downs.

The next morning Q and Betty set out on foot along Polurrian cliffs towards Mullion Cove to take a look at the house and here they found Henscath, an Edwardian villa built around 1903. It appeared to be a long bungalow-cum-house with a deep roof and dormer windows. A verandah with a corrugated roof ran across the front of the house. The walls were pebble dashed. They could only peep through the bushes and windswept sycamores but what they saw they liked very much. The views from here over the brooding moors sea and Mullion island were stunning and having looked no further they decided just from the outside that they had found their home.

They travelled into Helston to register their interest with the agent who would be dealing with the house and were even prepared to put up a deposit there and then. After all the war surely must end soon?

On their last morning they took the car down to the Cove for one last look at the harbour and Henscath before returning to London.

Approaching Mullion Cove by road you come to a large, now disused, quarry which serves as a convenient car park. Here the road divides into two, one road continuing straight down to the little harbour itself while the other winds and rises steeply, ending in a wide space outside the imposing Mullion Cove Hotel. This is as far as you can go as you have also reached the cliff edge, next stop the statue of Liberty. Here is the wide vista of the fabulous Mounts Bay where on a clear day you can just make out the form of St Michael's Mount in Marazion.

Henscath is about a hundred yards before that edge. A grassy path comes down to the road from the front of the house but to achieve the back of the house and park, there is a right angled turn to be made into an even steeper lane and half way up this lane is the entrance to the back yard and back garden. The lane carries on to a block of coastguard cottages. No doubt back in the nineteenth century Trinity House had made a splendid road of it but nothing had been done to it since, so that it consisted of enormous ruts and potholes between the original base of large lumps of granite. The condition of the lane was no aid to the difficult manoeuvres required to make the right angled turn into the back yard.

With their decision reaffirmed they set off back to London and whatever new fortunes the war may bring. Their quick decision to live in Cornwall especially on my mother's part was most probably fuelled by the uncertainty felt by everyone at that time. It was still a strong possibility that Hitler would invade, people lived their lives at a fast pace, lived their lives for now.

The war was to last another three harrowing years and when Betty became pregnant early in 1944, they decided to return to Luton for the duration of the rest of the war.

My older sister Wendy was born in the September of that year and now Q took up his position again at La Porte Industries and commuted to London two or three times a week to give lectures.

Finally in May 1945 the interminable war ended in Europe.

The RAF officers had vacated Henscath and Q gave in his notice to a very surprised Chairman. As he left his office the Chairman told him he would give him two years and then offer him his job back when he had got Cornwall out of his system. True to his word he was to make that offer two years to the day.

And so in September 1945, four months after the end of World War II in Europe, and with Wendy now aged one year, they packed up life in Luton to move to the large house overlooking Mullion Cove, much to the amazement of friends and family who were thoroughly sceptical about their departure over three hundred and twenty miles to the other end of the country. Nowadays of course with computers and technology and with instant communication possible, no one would think much about moving anywhere in the world but in the forties even moving as far as Cornwall was a very daring and unusual thing to do.

Prior to moving in, Q had managed one more quick visit to Henscath. He had been assured that the personnel occupying the house were 'officers and gentlemen' and the house would be clean and tidy but the walls belied this as they were decorated with most, to use my father's words, 'ungentlemanly' graffiti and the whole place was a decrepit mess. The everlasting damp for which Cornish houses are notorious had got to work since the house had been evacuated and produced some amazing growths of mould and fungus here and there, together with falls of plaster from walls and ceilings. The lofts were filled with collapsible metal beds painted blue or cream with horsehair mattresses, the large garden was totally overgrown.

Fortunately the Government had undertaken to restore the house to normal, fill in the various gun-pits and trenches in the garden and generally make the place habitable again.

The decoration was to be carried out as my parents wished and they made arrangements with a local builder. Now in those days the Cornish had a great passion for chocolate-brown paint inside their houses and a visit during the winter revealed that the decorator had managed to interpret the light colours chosen by my parents, as the said chocolate-brown. No doubt paint at that time was expensive and difficult to come by, perhaps someone had done a deal on brown paint. The effect as I remember my father saying, would have 'driven them and any future guests to 'melancholy madness'.

Fortunately there was still time to have the whole place repainted before they moved in.

They arrived finally at Henscath house in a large Morris Cowley shooting brake, and a Riley pathfinder, stuffed to the gunwales with belongings, followed closely by a large pantechnicon filled with furniture. Goodness knows how they managed to get enough petrol for the journey as it was still rationed but somehow they achieved it.

It never fails to surprise me even now, after years of driving from Sussex to Cornwall, just how far it is. As you come across the signs to Exeter there is a feeling of excitement at having reached the West Country but in fact there is still a long way to go, a hundred plus miles to the tip of the Cornish peninsula past such obscurely named places as Indian Queens, Truro, Playing Place, Devoran, Perranarworthal and the Norway Inn where my sister and I would screech at our father to go fast over the big hump on the bridge which we called the Norway Bump, now considerably flattened, then Long Downs with its old mines and frequent mists, towards the top of the old market town of Helston. Only nine miles to go now, along the road which cuts Culdrose Naval airbase in half, high fences with coils of vicious barbed wire along the top making it very plain that the civilian is not welcome there.

There are three different approaches after Culdrose to Mullion village. You can carry straight on the Lizard road until the turn off for Mullion at Penhale. There is a narrow road, virtually single carriage full of blind bends and with high Cornish hedges most of the way, but the road I always take is the turn off towards Cury just after Culdrose. Down through Nantithet valley with its very pretty well tended gardens, always full of colourful flowers in the summer. Over the now dry ford and up into Cury, past the big Methodist church. By now the traveller is aware that he is nearly at journey's end but has only had the occasional glimpse of sea and so as you pass the golf links and round the bend at the top of Poldhu past the windswept cedar trees, the spectacle which suddenly looms in front of your eyes is breath taking. Poldhu beach, one of the three Mullion beaches, presents itself proudly. A good sandy surfing beach flanked by high jagged cliffs. The imposing Poldhu hotel, now a nursing home, sits on one promontory which is also the spot from which Guglielmo Marconi sent the first radio signals to St. John's in Newfoundland in December 1901. The sky looks big here and a wide shallow stream snakes down the beach from under a narrow road bridge which you will pass over soon. The sea is ever changing but on a hot sunny day, the blue is startling as is the white foam that caresses the shore line. It is a very busy beach in summer as it is so accessible from the road and the car park in the valley but there is always a nook to be found amongst the rocks and rock pools. The road down to Poldhu is steep and winds back inland a little way following the contours of the grassy hummocks at the top of the beach before climbing up the other side and on towards Mullion village. Of course, the village has changed in several ways since the 1940s but it still retains its character. Mullion village as my parents would have found it in the forties, was compact, self-sufficient and charming, a main street which contained the shops, post office and banks and which suddenly narrows alarmingly for several yards between ancient white washed buildings until it widens out again to a junction to the right of which takes you past the main church and the Old Inn then back round to the village again, or branching off to the left to take you ultimately after a mile to Mullion Cove.

Half way to the Cove is a road on the right, known locally as Polurrian Turn and it was along there that Q and Betty drove on their first visit together, then out onto the rough unmade road along the top of Polurrian cliffs to Journeys End. They must have been exhausted after such a long journey and their ordeal at Penzance. And so the wagons arrived. The pantechnicon was barely able to turn up

the lane never mind into the right angled
gateway which lead to the back yard. The
neighbours up the lane were sympathetic
considering they were now completely
hemmed in until such time as the big
vehicle was emptied but in fact few had
cars anyway at that time.

Henscath was an unusual house in design,
although there were dormer windows in
the roof neither quite a dormer bungalow
nor a full house. There were two
staircases, one rising up from the lounge
hall in the centre of the house and one
near the kitchen at the top of the corridor.
Upstairs were four bedrooms, two of which
had normal square sash windows looking
out onto the spectacular scenery and two
of which had small dormer windows too
high to see comfortably out of. There was
a large bathroom and a separate loo.
Downstairs the stone flagged kitchen and
scullery-come-cloakroom were at one end
of the house , the lounge at the other end.
Doors to seven other rooms lead off the
long narrow corridors, only broken by the
large lounge hall.

There were five entrances to the house, a
back door from the kitchen, a middle and
a front door on either side of the lounge
hall and a door in each of the lounge and
dining room leading out at opposite ends
on to the verandah.

At last all of the contents were placed in the house and the pantechnicon drove away back up country.

Waking up on that first morning, my parents would have heard the roll of the sea, the loud high pitched caa-waaing of seagulls and the jackdaws squabbling at the top of the chimneys. And the quietness. Waking to quietness after being used to traffic noise, planes, sirens, slamming doors etc. is, I have found, surprisingly hard to get used to, it's almost as if your ears are waiting on the edge for the cacophony to begin. I can only try to imagine those first few days but it must have all seemed very strange exciting and possibly a bit scary to have finally arrived in that large damp house on the most south westerly tip of England. It was September and the nights were beginning to get chilly, no central heating and only a strange Dalek like cast iron boiler in the kitchen to heat the water. The boiler and my father became arch enemies pretty quickly but it remained the only source of heating the water for all of the time that we lived there. It was round ugly, functional, although that was debatable , and battleship grey and sat in the inglenook in the kitchen. It ran on anthracite, that being the cheapest form of coal at the time and although it had a

built in chimney, it was hard to tell if the wind was in the wrong direction, as smoke belched all over the kitchen and the back door and windows had to be opened even on the coldest of days. It was best to make a hasty retreat from the kitchen at those times, partly in order not to become asphyxiated but also so as not to hear my father's wrath as he tried to turn the pall of smoke from the damp fuel into flames. The Daily Telegraph and the Mirror were used for fire lighters, a page rolled into a tube and then coiled up and tucked in, in order to prolong their burning time and hopefully coax the damp anthracite to catch light. I remember helping to make those paper nuggets and reading eye catching old headlines and the adults comic strips, Jane, Garth and Tarzan in the Mirror as I did so. It was interesting to see that these two apposite newspapers that my parents took, evoked so much interest amongst their friends. There would be comments about the Mirror being 'a rag' and why on earth did they take it if they had the Telegraph but you could be sure that if the two papers were side by side on the kitchen table, it would always be the Mirror that was picked up and flicked through cover to cover.
I can imagine them on that first morning, breakfasting in the kitchen with Wendy in

her wooden high chair. Coaxing that boiler into life. Wandering through all the rooms upstairs and down and making mental notes, then taking a tour of the garden, still a bit of a wilderness at that time but a project which my father was keen to get on with. His dreams of growing all their own fruit and vegetables and becoming a bit of a market gardener certainly were to come true.   Life at Henscath had begun.

CHAPTER TWO

First Guests
1945-1947

By Christmas 1945 my parents were well settled into the house. My father reading volumes on market gardening, something he had never even considered before, my mother making the house into a home again after the RAF officers had left. Red felt carpets were laid, felt being more available just after the war and cheaper than other forms of carpet and the chimneys were swept. Long runs of walls were re-plastered and distempered. New furniture was designed and ordered, huge armchairs and settees and bespoke dining room furniture along with the furniture brought down from their house in Luton. It soon began to dawn on my parents that although they had a reasonable nest egg to live on for the moment, it certainly wasn't going to last for ever, especially with all the alterations and work that needed to be done in the house. But what to do? Cornwall at that time hardly abounded in the sort of industry and commerce in which they were experienced. In fact it was one of its charms that it did not. They looked around for activities which did provide a living for the local population.

Fishing hardly seemed their cup of tea, market gardening was a possible and an attractive thought but judging from the books he was reading, my father realised it would be quite a steep learning curve if they were to start making money from it soon. The idea of taking on some livestock was appealing but again their experience of animal husbandry was nil. Then it occurred to them that they had been 'customers' of the holiday industry. Why not start a guest house? With the ending of the war there was bound to be a boom in holiday making. Perhaps it was fortunate that it did not occur to them that running a guest house, like every other business, called for experience and special knowledge but it was decided and they started planning for it.

The guest house venture would wait until the summer of 1947 as my mother was still quite new to motherhood and adjusting to a very different life style. There would be a lot to consider and make ready for the taking in of guests.   By present day standards or perhaps even by 1940's standards, the house was not really ideal for a guest house. There was no central heating and no running water in the bedrooms. There were two bathrooms to be shared by six bedrooms and the hot water for these and the kitchen was supplied entirely by the temperamental old Tortoise boiler in the kitchen but they were not deterred and forged ahead optimistically with the idea.

And so tables, beds, bed side cabinets, white linen tablecloths and napkins, cutlery, crockery and bed linen and all the rest of the paraphernalia required for the guest house was slowly acquired over the year. There was also a very fine little silver art Deco gong resembling a young boy holding up a square of parchment. The gong to be rung when meals were ready.

Meanwhile my father having digested the tomes of gardening books, managed to acquire a small area of land in the grounds of the Blue Peter Club, a private, members only social club with a bar in the village, which he rented for a small sum. He had decided to try his hand at growing anemones which he hoped to send up to Covent Garden market. The mild climate was perfect for growing these vibrant colourful little flowers. It was hard work preparing the field, the earth was rough and full of stones which needed to be removed but he persisted and at last he was able to sow the corms, then wait and watch, weeding carefully between the rows until the first new shoots appeared.

He was lucky that first year and all his hard work paid off, the field produced a huge crop of flowers which with the help of willing village friends, were picked at the critical moment just before bloom and packed into large shallow heavy cardboard boxes with air holes and sent by train to Covent Garden market, beginning their journey by bus from Mullion, then steam train from Helston station, sadly no longer in existence due to the Beeching cuts in the Sixties. The flowers made a tidy little profit but the season was very short and it was a dicey business because one unexpected heavy frost could wipe out a whole crop as my father found to his cost on a few occasions.

By the winter of the following year of 1946 a significant change happened in the house. My father's life time best friend Ron came to stay at Henscath after losing his wife Sheila to the lung disease tuberculosis. TB as it was known, was still a major threat to many lives at that time and the medicines to treat it still in their infancy. The BCG vaccine although invented before the first world war, was only available to those considered to be at the greatest risk. Ron was completely devastated and seemed unable to move on, he and Sheila had only been married for two or three years and for much of that time Sheila had been affected by the disease.

Ron was still living in Luton and had also lost many of his family peers in the war. My parents suggested he come to stay at Henscath for a few months and he could help out with the guest house for which they would give him a small income as well as his board and lodging.

And so Ron arrived...... and stayed for ten years. He was a fine looking man but was afflicted by an absolute terror of dentists and when he smiled there were several teeth missing or broken and he must have been in a lot of pain at times but there it was and no amount of encouragement would ever have got him to go for treatment. Looking back I think I regarded him as a sort of second father as by the time I was born in 1948, Ron was as much a part of the household as everyone else and he assumed the title of Uncle to Wendy and me. I remember after saying my prayers at night, it was God bless Mummy God bless Daddy God bless Wendy and God bless Uncle Ron, which was what sealed the family for me.

Saying prayers, kneeling at the foot of the bed before climbing in at night seemed to be the universal thing that kids did in the fifties, certainly all our friends, whatever the beliefs of our parents, it's just a habit that children were taught to do like brushing their teeth.

With Ron now on board, recovering slowly and eager to offer any help he could, the garden began to take shape and vegetables were planted. Ron and my father set about erecting a large greenhouse in the back garden where they would experiment with various plants which might become commercially viable and salad plants which would also be useful for the guest menu.

Henscath was still looking fresh from its Government make-over and the efforts and new furnishings Betty and Q had put into it and Ron had his furniture delivered to the house which surely must have indicated that he intended staying for more than a few months.   His furniture included a grand piano which luckily was able to be accommodated into the large lounge at the end of the house, not really a prime requirement for a guest house but again it was something that was always there through my young childhood. I remember standing at one end of the keyboard just able to peep over while Ron played jazz. Was he any good? I don't know but I loved it and was fascinated and I'm sure it was what started me on my lifetime love of all music, with the exception oddly, of jazz. When he finished playing he would lift me onto the piano stool so I could tinker around the notes. I was a little scared of the huge black lid that hovered over the working parts of the piano and was always glad when it was closed. Ron was also able to provide chairs and a few beds and tables and a small knight in shining armour which stood by the fireplace. Another of Uncle Ron's odd pieces of furniture was known as the Alfred. I have never seen or heard of such a piece of furniture since but it was of large footstool size, the top, covered in dark leather and of basket weave, sat on top of the short legs in the shape of a half circle. It was useful for pretending to be on horseback but possibly very little else. At last all was made ready for the first guest house season which started in the June of 1947. The first guests arrived along with another very sharp learning curve of cooking and hosting, both of which my parents appeared to achieve with relative ease. My mother becoming a very fine cook indeed over the years, unaided in that department by my father who until the end of his days was barely able to boil an egg. It must have been a nerve wracking time taking strangers into your house for the first time, feeding them good food and making their stay a memorable occasion. I have the first log of visitors still. The first names to appear in the book being one N. Grocott from St Georges Avenue Westcliff-On-Sea Essex and JD Britten from Marguerite Drive Leigh-On-Sea Essex Nationality: English, Date of arrival 31.5.1947, Date of departure 07.6.1947 How I wish there was any further information other than that flat entry into the book. There is no mention of them being either male or female, friends or family but there they are, the first arrivals and I hope they enjoyed their stay. They were followed on the 7th June by a Mr. and Mrs. Clayton from London N10 and a Mr. and Mrs. Lloyd on the 8th June. Several of the guests that first year came in the form of our family and friends who wanted to come and see how my parents were getting on in their new choice of lifestyle. They must have been very pleasantly relieved to find that my parents were settled and happy, with what seemed to be a thriving little business going on. The tariff for a stay including breakfast and evening meal was nine guineas a week per person, the equivalent of £9.45 now. Even then this was considered to be an extremely reasonable price. Eventually they raised it to ten guineas or £10.50. It does not really equate to today's money as it was pre decimal and therefore in shillings and pence, the guinea being worth twenty one shillings, the pound being worth twenty shillings.

The little silver gong was rung at eight fifty for breakfast at nine, breakfast was cooked by my mother served by my father and washed up by Ron. Most people did not stay for lunch but occasionally a few light lunches were served and picnics packed together for taking on trips. In the evening the gong was rung for dinner at seven as the Archers finished on the radio. Busy times but my mother always made it look easy and was unruffled by the constant flow of local visitors who seemed to feel the need to sit around the kitchen table consuming cups of tea at any given time of the day, reading the papers or making somewhat unhelpful comments about how my mother should be running her kitchen but there was a lot of laughter too. The guests who were relaxed on their holiday would stand for ages chatting to my mother in the corridors and she always found time for a conversation. I wish it was possible to recapture the conversations around that kitchen table. I remember little snippets of them but that's all. At the weekends out of tourist season, the cups of tea around the table were replaced by alcohol and thick acrid smoke from Players and Capstan full strength cigarettes and my father's pipe. If the old boiler happened to be playing up at the time as well belching its own smoke into the room, all windows and outside doors were flung open, it must have been as thick as a London smog.

It was a sad fact that neither of my parents had much in the way of business acumen and although the guest house provided enough to just about get by, there were lean times in the winters that followed. It is only a relatively recent thing that many people take several holidays each year; in the forties and fifties, apart from the fact that there was not much money around for leisure spending, annual leave was often restricted to one week per year; two if you were very lucky and taking a winter break in England was almost unheard of. The holiday industry in those days had a fairly specific and short season from early May to the beginning of September and most people who took in guests needed to supplement their income over the winter months with another source of revenue hence in my father's case, the growing of anemones but the anemone season was short and the last guests departed in early September.

Despite my parents foray into market gardening, and running the guest house, it seemed that their financial situation was not improving sufficiently especially with the addition of one more adult to feed. One of the cars had to go leaving them with the rather temperamental wooden framed Morris Cowley shooting brake which being a utility vehicle was much more fit for purpose than the beautiful Pathfinder. The trouble was that any profit made throughout the short summer months had to tide them through the winter. It seemed that another venture was going to have to be found, made more urgent by the fact that my mother became pregnant with me in the September of 1947.

My parents were sitting in the Old Inn one night chatting to David and Joan over the bar, it came up in conversation that their supplier of delicious Cornish pasties was no longer able to carry on his business. The Old Inn's pasties were much sought after so this was quite a blow. My mother mentioned casually that she might like to have a go at making them and it was agreed that she should try. In retrospect I would have thought that running a guest house and bringing up a child would have taken most of her time but she was full of energy in those days and up for a challenge.

As with most things, it did not take her

long to master the art of pasty making but she realised early on that she would need the help of my father and perhaps Ron as well if she was going to be making one or two dozen a day. I make them now occasionally and find it very time consuming and messy just to make a few. The pasty making started at six in the morning on the scrubbed wooden table in the kitchen. My father in charge of peeling the potatoes and onions and swede and then mincing them in a big metal mincer attached to the table. Underneath the mincer was a large saucepan on the floor to catch the liquid and starch that was squeezed out of the vegetables. I loved the smell of the raw vegetables and sticking my fingers into the starchy goo that filled the saucepan. Whilst this happened my mother started on the pastry making. Into a huge china bowl went the flour lard and Echo margarine which then had to be rubbed together before pouring in ice cold water and turning the whole thing into a very large lump of ready pastry. Then the rolling and cutting out six rounds at a time with a saucepan lid. Onto these went potato swede chuck steak or skirt the whole thing finally topped with onion. Lots of salt and pepper sprinkled on each layer. The pastry was then folded over the contents enclosing them by sticking the edges together with the aid of a light brushing of milk and then skilfully twisting the edges into the heavy crust that classically forms the top of a Cornish pasty. By seven am the pasties were smelling delicious in a hot oven and as soon as cold enough were packed into the anemone boxes which turned out to be the perfect containers for them. My father would then go to meet the bus at the end of the lane where he would hand the boxes over to the bus conductor to be met outside the Old Inn by David who would be waiting to collect them. The pasties were a great success and the making of them went on for several more years. Work over the summer period was unending, seven days a week and my parents rarely got to bed until late. Their respite being to lie in bed and listen to the late edition of the Goon shows which they both loved.

Very occasionally there would be the odd day or evening over summer when there were no guests to worry about and if it coincided with a Sunday when there were never any pasties made, the family would go out in the Cowley, perhaps to Kynance cove or Porthleven or walk from the bottom of Helston through the beautiful Penrose estate valley to Loe bar, the largest fresh water lake in Cornwall separated from the sea by a shingle bank. More often it would be to the sandy coves nearby, through the cave from Mullion harbour where you could warm your back against a polished serpentine rock on the beach or along the cliffs to Polurrian beach where the smooth slate fallen from the cliff made useful seating.

Once the last of the visitors had left in mid-September, a sigh of relief went around the village, grateful though everyone was for their bookings, no more coach loads of visitors, sometimes there would be four or five coaches at a time parking up by the hotel while their passengers, locally known as Emmets or Grockles, poured down the cliff paths to the harbour. Gone were the cars, the ice creams and the buckets and spades. There were beautiful days in late Autumn and during the winter months when the coves were reclaimed. Kynance, packed over the summer with sun worshipping holiday makers draped over the warm shiny serpentine rocks, was deserted and local people delighted in having it back to themselves. Often when we visited Kynance on a warm sunny day over the winter months, always with a picnic and a thermos flask, we would have the whole place to ourselves. Poldhu beach which also was always packed with families due to its easy access, and whose name means 'black pool' in the Cornish language , took on a completely different atmosphere over the winter months, open and brooding.

It was during these months that the family enjoyed exploring the world around them. One favourite haunt was the Helford river. French trading boats once brought rum and tobacco to Helford when it was an important port. That of course was long ago and for many years it was just a small sleepy fishing village. Daphne Du Maurier who had lived at Henscath for a while as a child, wrote the romantic novel, Frenchman's Creek around Helford where she had spent her honeymoon. It is indeed a romantic and beautiful place as are the many creeks and hamlets which cluster on its shores. Now it is a haven for the rich and famous and most of the houses lie unused in Helford village for many months of the year. Whilst this has to a great extent taken away the heartbeat of day to day living and community life in Helford, its charm has not been spoiled.

For me the most magical place on the Helford lying in Gillan creek, is St Anthony with its imposing church and small cluster of houses. The peaceful shady graveyard at the rear of the church tells many sad stories of lives lost at sea. The water on this tidal estuary is as clear as crystal and there is a mixture of soft grey sand and flat pebbles, ideal for skimming and small yellow shells, a must for collecting by small children to stick on trinket boxes or to keep in a jar. When the tide is right out and the boats are lying on their sides at their moorings, there is dark green sea weed clinging to the small boulders and muddy blackness but the sea is out there sparkling green blue, waiting to return and it is an almost spiritual experience to sit for a day watching the water drift gently back in, lifting the boats back up to float again and lapping the shoreline. The mood changes and the stunning beauty returns. From St Anthony you can look across to Gillan beach with its pretty blue and white houses and grassy headlands. You can reach the beach by boat or from the land side by an unmade steep leafy lane which passes pretty houses on the way.

And so the first summer season came to an end in September. It had been more successful than my parents and Ron could have imagined but there was still a nagging doubt in my father's mind as to whether the guest house, the anemone growing and the pasty making were going to sustain the family throughout a whole year and it was tough and constant work. There was no guarantee that the guest house would always be full or that the anemone crop would be successful which added further strain. Added to that, the advent of my birth would mean another mouth to feed.

Wendy was now three years old and schooling needed to be considered. There was a village primary school, now the post office, and another tiny school opposite the church hall, run by a delightful elderly spinster lady, Miss Mitchell and it was to this school that Wendy would be sent but it was already being rumoured that Miss Mitchell was nearing retirement and wishing to turn her house back into a residential dwelling. Wendy at this early stage was also showing a strong desire to dance, from the moment she could walk she would go up on to her toes and dance whenever there was music on the radio to dance to. There was a small ballet school in the village run by a lady called Nickie Nicholson in the Womens' Institute on a Saturday morning. Wendy went to ballet lessons there from the age of three and straight away Nickie saw that she had a very talented child to nurture and would be instrumental in Wendy's ballet training later on.

Another idea was beginning to hatch in my father's mind. How about starting a small private school themselves? The seed was planted and began to grow. My father had been an outstanding pupil at Luton grammar school. He had matriculated a year earlier than was normal with top marks in every subject. Sadly in those long ago days the idea of going to university was probably not even discussed in his family and he went straight out to work at La Porte Industries where luckily his talents were quickly recognised and he rose to management at an early age. Nevertheless with his command of his favourite subjects English language and English literature, he may have forged a very different career had he gone to a university. Teaching did and still does feature heavily in our family and so the idea of starting his own school was by no means an odd one.

CHAPTER THREE

I am Born
1947 – 1948

Growing up with the sea at my feet was paradise for me and being near water, be it river lake or sea, is where I always feel my spirits rise. There were many beach days in those early years and in all seasons. In high summer Kynance cove was very busy with all the visitors and locals who were prepared to climb the hazardous routes down steep stony cliff paths, to spend a day sitting on the sand against the warm smooth serpentine rocks and sitting in or wading through the deep warm pools left when the tide had withdrawn and just marvelling at the beauty of the place. The sea around Kynance takes on a particular bright deep blue/green colour and moves in at different angles around the rocks, wonderful for swimming as long as you are careful. You had to keep an eye on the tide though as you could easily find yourself cut off from the cliff path and many a little group of people were to be seen wading quickly through water around a rock with soaking belongings and fractious children, so as not to be marooned at the top of the beach waiting for the next low tide.

The little café nestling at the back of the cove, its supplies brought in by Land Rover down an almost impenetrable steep track, was bursting at the seams.

There were no wet suits or stand up surf boards or many of the other sea toys available now, so other than a few intrepid swimmers in swimming trunks and bathing costumes, the sea did not invite people in during the autumn and winter in those days.

The south west tip of Cornwall invariably misses out on snow.

There are usually fierce storms at some point over the winter and if a gale reaches force nine or more, it is essential to stay indoors if possible. The Beaufort scale classifies force seven as moderate gale with winds of thirty two to thirty eight mph graduating through force eight and nine to ten which is storm/whole gale with winds of fifty five to sixty three mph. To walk out onto the cliffs would be foolishness as the wind could pull you over in an instant. The sea whips up into a fury but is fabulously dramatic to watch.

Mullion island inhabited only by sea birds, stands steadfastly out at sea half a mile from the harbour which it protects to some extent, its highest point being a hundred and eighteen feet above sea level. If the gale force is strong enough, the waves can break over the top of the island and the harbour is awash. It is a spectacular sight like foam being tossed around in a washing machine. Henscath usually suffered some form of damage from a particularly fierce storm. There were two occasions when the winds ripped out a dormer window which came crashing down on the corrugated iron roof of the verandah outside mine and Wendy's shared bedroom. There were some extraordinary results from the strength of the wind. The most spectacular and alarming damage we experienced at Henscath concerned some two hundred glass cloches set up on the vegetable patch behind the house. Late one afternoon while a pretty 'normal' gale was in progress, there was a sudden colossal boom and blast like a land mine going off. It transpired later that the wind speed had shot up from forty or so to ninety-five in seconds. Although cloches were apt to provide at least a few casualties in a gale, the effect of this was truly startling. Looking out of the kitchen window we could see dozens of them being lifted ten or fifteen feet into the air, the panes of glass separating and being hurled over the high Cornish hedge into our elderly neighbours garden. If anyone had walked up that garden path they would have had a good chance of being decapitated. My father rushed to the phone to warn them. Later on when inspecting the damage, we discovered one cloche had been picked up and deposited next door completely undamaged.

But for all that drama from wind and rain, snow is a rarity in the extreme South West, the climate being milder than up country, in fact I can only remember snow on a handful of occasions and usually it didn't last long and so the extreme cold of the winter of 1947 would have come as a surprise to everyone. It was miserable, power cuts, blocked roads and high winds causing major snow drifts. It was the coldest winter on record with temperatures said to have plummeted to -22%, although the lowest recorded was at Exeter airport where it was -16%.

Many people were marooned for weeks. Henscath, high on a hill and draughty at the best of times must have given its occupants their fair share of misery. No central heating and of course no double glazing. Hard to visualise how uncomfortable it could be when the only warmth was when you were huddled by a fire with cold draughts coming in from every nook and cranny, of which there seemed to be very many in Henscath.

There was something about the cold in
Cornwall that seemed to get into your very
bones. Winters were cold and damp and
anything left for a while without being
moved, gained a fur coat of mould. Shoes
went mouldy and the shoe polish gained a
film of mould. There was mould around
the windows and even some books were
not spared. Our beds were piled high with
wool blankets but even they felt a little
damp sometimes. We had heavy stone hot
water bottles at our feet and a rubber hot
water bottle to hug. If the stone hot
water bottle fell out of the bed during the
night it woke you up with the crash.
I don't remember my parents speaking of
that winter but knowing how miserable
just a normal cold damp winter could be
there as a child, they surely must have
wondered if the move had been a big
mistake. That winter may have been the
reason for the abhorrence I have always
had for being cold. Given the choice I
would always rather be too warm.
The winter of 1947 dragged on into March
1948 when the temperatures changed
dramatically causing the snow to melt
quickly and there was major flooding all
over the country. Flooding was not a
concern for my parents as they were
situated so high but they were in the full
face of the violent gales that followed.

I was due to be born in March of 1948, on the same day in fact that Joan Truscott from the Old Inn was due to have her baby but although Nicholas arrived quite punctually, I decided to wait another three weeks and at last it was time for my father to phone the local midwife to attend. The local midwife was Auntie Nellie, not a real aunt of course but that's what we kids all called her. She lived in one of the cluster of terraced houses in the lee of the cliff just up from the harbour. Auntie Nellie was a wonderful character, she had long hair which she plaited and rolled up on the back of her head Swiss maid style. She came from London and was proud to be a Cockney. She was married to Glen, one of the local fishermen, most of whose family also lived in the cove. I can only imagine that they met when she had come on holiday to Mullion. Like my mother, there must have been a few raised eyebrows when the young Nellie announced she was to marry and go to live in Cornwall.   I remember Nellie's mother coming to stay on occasions, an austere looking old lady dressed in black with a deeply wrinkled and weathered face . She would sit out on the little lawn at the front of the house staring out at the view for hours.
Nellie and Glen had one daughter but

sadly she died as a young child. The little girl's photograph was up on the mantel piece above the Rayburn and I never heard Nellie or Glen speak of her.

The house was so close to the lee of a cliff at the back, that there was room only for a narrow concrete path to the back door, there was always water trickling down through the vegetation of the cliff and into man made gulleys on the path. As a young child I would pop in there quite often with one or other of my parents when they went to buy their cigarettes as one of Auntie Nellie's little outlets was the selling of tobacco. I only ever saw their main living area, coming in through the back door you were faced with a very dark winding staircase. As a child I longed to know what was up there but never dared to ask. I remember wondering in the ghoulish way that children do, if their little daughter was lying up there in her bed. The main living room was warm and inviting. A large dark wooden grandfather type cuckoo clock towered against one wall. Under the window which looked out through other clustered houses across the harbour to the sea, stood an old chaise longue and several other odd pieces of furniture. A large sweetie jar stood on the mantel and my eye always roved to make sure it was still there because I knew as we were leaving it would be taken down so Wendy and I could choose a sweetie to take home. It was always warm and cosy in that room and if we happened to arrive around lunch time, Uncle Glen a small wiry man with startlingly blue alert eyes, would sit me on his knee and allow me a bite of his Cornish pasty. A treat indeed. I remember he smelled very strongly of fish sitting there in his navy blue Breton jumper with his cap perched on the back of his head and a huge mug of dark strong sweet tea close by. I was offered a sip of that sometimes but it was usually too hot. If we were lucky we would get to hear the cuckoo announce the hour. I marvelled at the little bird and wondered how it knew how to tell the time and I loved to watch the long pendulum as it moved gently from side to side tocking quietly as it went.

So Auntie Nellie was called in and on the 11th April 1948 she delivered me in Henscath in room number four upstairs. Because I was actually born in Cornwall I had the automatic right to be Cornish and so was the only member of my family who did not have to wait the regulation twenty five years before being accepted as a Cornish resident.

My earliest memories are of being in a huge black pram on the verandah and seeing faces peering in at me or do I just think those are memories having seen photos and heard people talking but I think they are.

Due to my being born in April my parents decided not to take in guests for that year until July to give my mother a little time to recover and give her whole attention to looking after me and Wendy for a few months. This gave another blow to the income for the household and added to that the anemone crop was very poor due to the winter that had preceded their growing. Only the pasty making continued as soon as my mother was properly back on her feet again.

The hard work my father and Ron put into the vegetable patch began to reap rewards which was a great help towards the expense of meals and although the guest season started late, Henscath was full from July to late in September when Wendy, now aged four, began school in the village with Miss Mitchell as her teacher.

It was around this time that the family acquired their first dog, a brindle bull terrier who established himself well up the pecking order from the day he arrived at Henscath.

He was around six months old when my father appeared home with him one

Sunday lunch time after a visit to the Old Inn where he had got chatting to a young man from Gweek. The young man was looking for a new home for Bruno and was prepared to swap him for the price of a couple of pints of Cornish. His eagerness to be rid of the dog should have set a few warning bells in my father's head but the deal was done and Bruno marched bandy legged into the kitchen, surveyed the scene and squatted for a long pee right in the middle of the stone floor.

Bruno had no notion of boundaries, as big as the garden was, his need for freedom was paramount and at every opportunity he would make a bolt for the lane, often with my father in hot pursuit until the dog's mouse like tail disappeared round the corner at the bottom of the hill.

It was usually after about an hour that the telephone would ring. It might be from the butcher's shop where Bruno had paid a quick visit and disappeared with sausages or a chop. Or he may have nipped into someone's kitchen, terrorised their cat and polished off the cat food. Sometimes he had got into someone's garden and made amorous advances, sometimes conquests, on their precious pooch. All very embarrassing and the list went on and on until Bruno had made quite a name for himself in the village.

Eventually his adventures had to be curtailed and he was hooked by a ring at the end of his lead, to the washing line where he could run up and down and then sit looking very mournful and cry so pathetically that someone would eventually take pity on him and unhook the lead, whereupon with a mad glint in his eye he would make another bolt for freedom.

Bruno's comeuppance was a very scary moment which fortunately none of the family were there to see. One of his greatest passions was to chase cattle, which was certainly not to be recommended. He was very adept at rounding them up and cornering them in the field until the inevitable phone call from a blood boiling farmer, who probably had every right to turn his shotgun on him. Once again my father had to try to smooth the ruffled feathers with a few promised pints in the pub and assurances that it wouldn't happen again which of course it did.

As summer approached and grass became lush everywhere, cattle were put out to graze on the cliffs. It was one hot afternoon when Bruno managed to bite through his restricting lead hooked to the clothes line and make his getaway, unnoticed for the moment.

It was quite some time later when a bloodied limping Bruno dragged himself slowly through the open gate and collapsed in the back yard, followed by Jimmy, a young lad from the village, who wanted to make sure that he had made it home.

My concerned parents rushed to mop him up and tend to the deep wounds on his body and head, give him a few laps of water and place him carefully in his basket by the boiler.

Then tea was made and they all sat around the kitchen table to hear what had happened from Jimmy. Apparently Bruno was heading down the cliff path towards Polurrian beach. As he approached the wide flatter grass half way down, he spied a dozen or so Guernsey and Friesian (not known for their good humour) cows grazing near the edge of the cliff.

Jimmy was heading to the beach for a swim at the same time and saw the whole awful incident that followed. Bruno had leapt into action barking ferociously and rounding up the bunch of cattle, guiding them inexorably towards the edge of the cliff. Jimmy and a couple of holiday makers who were also witnessing the impending disaster, bravely tried to get themselves between the cattle and the cliff edge to steer them back but it was no use and they were obliged to move quickly out of the way as the cattle surged towards them, there seemed only one possible horrendous conclusion.

One cow, well ahead of the others reached the edge and her front legs slipped over the side landing by great good fortune, on a small ledge. At that moment a particularly large Friesian member of the herd stopped in her tracks and turned her head towards the dog. The rest of the herd panicked and briefly stopped the charge towards their doom. Bruno stood his ground trying to force the poor creatures forward but the large bovine was having none of it.

Jimmy got very excited as he recounted what happened next.

The angry cow then made a charge towards the unsuspecting Bruno, gathering great speed and as she reached him, head down, picked him up on her horns like a feather and tossed him hard into the air, gouging his back as she did so. He landed forcibly on a small outcrop of rocks, badly winded and in great pain. The cows grouped together now and stared as cows do and Jimmy and the astonished holiday makers, ran to the dog, certain that he would be dead but found he was still breathing. They went to the aid of the struggling scared cow that needed help to get back onto the cliff and fortunately was none the worse for her unwanted adventure. By the time that was done, Bruno had managed to struggle to his feet and begin the long stagger home over the cliff path, no amount of coaxing from Jimmy would make him stop. It was a hard lesson but thank goodness Bruno had the sense to know when he was beaten and he never went near a cow again.

One morning Bruno again intent on escape turned up the lane for a change. This lead to the row of coastguard houses behind Henscath, no longer inhabited by coastguards but with local families in need of housing. Next to them were a couple of large bungalows and a little further on down a narrow rutted drive, a large imposing house called Trenoweth, white faced with an orange tiled roof.

As my father wearily pulled on his boots to give chase yet again to the errant dog, he saw an odd sight flash past the open back door, surely it was Bruno but something else too. My father went to the door only to discover that Bruno had arrived home with a pair of men's trousers.

"Oh no" my mother exclaimed "what on earth has he been up to now and what has he done with the owner?"

Should they phone the police? Should

they wait for an irate man to come by clad only in his underpants claiming the dog had wrestled him to the ground and run off with his trousers?

They decided to wait and see what happened – nothing did – no one seemed to have gone missing or reported a trouser thief.

A few days later Bruno returned from his wanderings, this time with a pair of men's underpants, they were slightly damp and had the unmistakable impressions of clothes peg marks on them. Oh dear, Bruno had now turned into a clothes line thief. The clothes were left out on the hedge for a week but no one ever claimed them. He received a good 'dressing' down and luckily seemed to decide that pinching clothes from clothes lines was not going to be appreciated and he dropped that particular vice.

It was several years later when Bruno had calmed down to some extent and stopped roaming the village, that a very different drama happened to him.

My mother had taken my sister on a clothes shopping day trip to Truro and left my surrogate Uncle Ron and my father in charge. They decided to tackle the overgrown hedges in the front garden and Bruno delighted in foraging amongst the undergrowth while they worked. Suddenly he let out the most terrible yelp, backing out of a clump of bracken. The yelping continued and the two men rushed to his side as he started to collapse. There on the side of his face were the unmistakable marks of a bite almost certainly from an adder.   Ron carried the flailing dog into the cool kitchen and laid him on the stone floor, his face now hideously swollen as he writhed in agony and began to fight for breath.

What to do? My mother had taken the car and anyway the vet was a good half an hour's drive away. Bruno didn't look as if he would last that long anyway. It was obvious he was going to die. My father hit upon the idea that to make his death less agonising, they would administer some brandy. They trickled a very hefty tot down the dog's throat and he seemed to calm a little. They gave him some more and placed him carefully on his bed as his breathing became more and more shallow. Wendy and my mother returned from their shopping trip and were very distressed to hear what had happened. At bedtime Wendy gave him a stroke and said her sad goodbyes.

The next morning Ron went to the kitchen ready to deal with a dead dog and was utterly astonished to find him now in a deep steady sleep, very much alive and

with the swelling dramatically down.
It seemed that the brandy had taken
Bruno to a quiet place where his body
could fight off the poisons that the adder
had inflicted.
Bruno lived to a ripe old age and for all his
naughtiness was a loving and loved dog.
The bookings for summer visitors were
rolling in quite fast and there were pupils
booked in for the start of the school in
September, my father turned his mind to
the keeping of livestock. He and Ron
considered growing pigs for bacon,
keeping chickens to supply the guest
house with eggs and ducks to be bred for
the table. They decided to try rearing
ducks first of all and after seeking advice
as always, they decided on buying two
dozen Aylesbury ducklings. The ducks
were perhaps the most amusing of all the
creatures who would arrive at Henscath
over the years as they all seemed to have
very individual personalities. Ron and my
father built a solid duck house and as
there was no water in the garden for
ducks to swim in, my father acquired a
long zinc bath with a plank propped at
either end. The ducks were quite comical
to watch as they would waddle in line up
one plank, plop into the water swim the
length of the bath, then down the plank at
the other end, only to repeat the

performance over and over again.
Because they were to be reared for the
table, the ducklings were all supposedly
drakes as eggs were not required.
Although the ducks were a very good
source of income, both Ron and my
father's utter loathing of killing any
animal, especially a full grown drake which
does not go easily; took its toll and
eventually they had to admit that they
could no longer take on that task. They
knew they would be ribbed locally for
having to admit defeat in the slaughtering
department but as usual there were plenty
of local hands willing to help them out.
It transpired that three of the ducks were
in fact female and after the rest of the
drakes had become welcome dishes with
slices of orange, the three females became
pets and as a reward they laid eggs fairly
regularly for a time.
Eventually the supply of eggs stopped
rather abruptly, too soon to be the natural
end of a laying batch.
Then my father noticed a peculiar thing.
When their food was put out by the back
door, invariably only two ducks would turn
up. These two never finished the food but
when they had had a good tuck in they
would start up a loud quacking and
squawking. Minutes later the third duck
would appear and one of the others would

vanish. Meantime we got no eggs.

The thing to do, obviously, was to track one of them, so this my father did, watching from the kitchen window one afternoon as the usual performance was repeated, he waited until the third duck appeared and one of the other ducks began its trek away from the food. It would have been a funny sight to see my father dodging from one point to another, trying to avoid being spotted by the wanderer as she waddled laboriously across the yard to the gate and up the lane blissfully unaware that my father was hot on her trail

Purposefully she waddled on past the back of the garages and the back of our immediate neighbours, the Ladner's house. Occasionally she would stop as if to get her bearings before purposefully setting off again. Each time she stopped, my father would take cover until she moved on again. Finally she veered off the path and started to make her way up the long rough drive leading to Trenoweth. Half way along the drive she stopped suddenly. My father only just managed to 'duck' down to avoid being seen as she looked round her and then turned into the undergrowth.

My father waited a few moments before following her in where he found her

squatting on as many as she could cover
of a collection of twenty seven eggs.
between them the three ducks had built
up the nest of eggs about two metres from
the side of the road in dense bracken
about three hundred yards from our
house. No doubt the intention was to
hatch them but they would have been out
of luck. Not only was it impossible for any
one of them to have covered so many
eggs but in any case the drakes had long
since gone and the chances of fertility
must have been nil. The ducks were never
replaced after they had lived out full lives.

Wendy with the ducks (Henscath)

Stormy day Mullion harbour

CHAPTER FOUR

Religious Wars and Lucifer
1948 – 1949

My father was becoming increasingly concerned about the financial situation and was beginning to wonder whether they should seriously reconsider moving back up country. It was now clear that Ron had no intention of leaving any time soon and there were two small children to look after. Whilst Cornwall was a wonderful place for children to grow up, was it really worth all this stress and worry and wondering where they were going to find the money to pay the bills? He recalled his thoughts on the possibility of starting their own school.

Soon after my birth he told my mother of his ideas. The plan would be that my mother would teach from age three to five or six years old and then my father would take the children through to the eleven plus entrance exam at ten or eleven years, after which the children would mostly move on to the Grammar school in Helston if they passed their eleven plus exam or the Secondary Modern school if they did not. The advent of the Comprehensive system was still a long way off. My mother would also cook for the children who stayed for lunch as well as make some lunches for any of the guest house guests who overlapped the school term. I cannot begin to know why she gave the idea any credence at all or how on earth she could possibly have thought she could add more to her extremely busy days, let alone with a new baby in the house but not only did she agree, she immediately threw herself into studying for her new role as teacher and planning the necessary changes that would need to be made to the house.

There would be much planning and studying to do and permissions obtained for the setting up of a school and so the decision was made to start in September of the following year 1949. Miss Mitchell's school was about to close for good which would mean moving Wendy from there to another school anyway and the other local village school was very oversubscribed so there was certainly a place for a new primary school albeit theirs would be quite small with a maximum of around twenty children.

There were official documents to be filled in and there would be an inspection of the facilities before they could begin. The large dining room would become my father's schoolroom during term times, reverting to a dining room for the long summer holidays for the holiday guests. One of the large bedrooms at the other end of the house would be used for the three to five year olds that my mother would teach. Where guests clashed with term times, a further bedroom next to the dining-cum-schoolroom would be used as the guests' dining room. The scullery next to the kitchen would easily turn into a cloakroom for the children. There were hooks around the walls and benches to sit on while the children changed into their indoor shoes.

Gradually over that summer and the next, all the paraphernalia for the school was acquired. Blackboards, chalk, exercise books, desks, chairs etc. and posters such as maps and past kings and queens of England to decorate the walls. Children's books were donated by friends and neighbours for a small school library. The two lawns were to become playgrounds, one for my mother's small children and one for the older children. Uncle Ron who was to have no part in the school other than helping in the kitchen with school lunches, would take on the responsibility of looking after me during the school hours.

At last the day arrived when the school inspector was to pay his visit. My parents were both very nervous as everything depended now on their being able to go ahead.

The inspector arrived, a small red faced man, daunted by the steepness of the hill and lane, he left his car in the quarry and walked up to the house. He arrived puffing and panting and my mother invited him into the kitchen for a cup of tea before he started his tour. My parents had met with much officiousness throughout the process so it was a great relief to meet this friendly pleasant man. Feeling refreshed after the tea he began his inspection of the school rooms, the cloakroom, the washing and toilet facilities and he checked the safety of the play areas. After that there was a rechecking of both my parents qualifications to teach children. It all took a long time and before he left, the inspector was grateful for more tea and biscuits but gave no indication whatsoever as to his findings with regard to the school. Finally he left and now it was waiting time. A day went by, a week and no communication at all. It began to feel that the school venture was not going to happen. Another two weeks went by and my father told my mother that now he really feared the worst, he could see no reason for the delay. Then the telephone rang, my father answered it and there on the end of the line was a man from the

education authority with the news that
they could go ahead and an official
document would be arriving in the post.
The relief was huge and there was a party
in the Old Inn that night to celebrate.
Mullion was to have a new school to start
in September 1949.

Now they could put their advertisement in
the West Briton newspaper and advertise
locally in the village, although being such
a small place, word of mouth probably got
around even more quickly.

The guest house was fully booked for the
summer and that coupled with pasty
making and two small children, thoughts
of teaching in September would have to be
put on the back burner for the moment.
My parents were 'incomers' and as such
had to serve a very long apprenticeship
before they could officially be accepted
into the community, so the idea of them
opening a school was going to be watched
very carefully. Not surprising really as a
small population living in a remote area
has a fragile structure and the smallest
change can tip the balance and the
dynamics of day to day living for
everyone. There have been a few
entrepreneurial 'incomers' to Mullion over
the years trying to give a more
commercial touristy feel to the village but
the resistance has been fierce and they

have tended to leave well alone and try
their luck elsewhere in the end thank
goodness. Most people reckoned it was
twenty five years before an incomer could
be accepted, never mind trying to force
sudden and unacceptable changes on the
village.

With that in mind my parents were careful
and content to abide by the rules and
make their way through what could be
quite a rocky course at times. The local
etiquette was not always easy to
understand and incomers were watched
carefully.

The village was mostly divided between
devout Methodists and Church of England,
there was also a small Roman Catholic
church on the fringe of the village. The
divide between the two main churches was
made all the greater by the fact that
Mullion Church of England was very 'High'
church. The incumbent vicar at the time,
one Father Harris, would waft through the
village in his white robes from the
vicarage which I found strangely scary as
a child. The procession inside the church
to the altar on a Sunday morning was
accompanied by much wafting of incense.
The strict Methodist population was by far
the greater and you could be certain that
the large Wesleyan chapel with its tall
imposing arched windows, would be full

for each Sunday service. Years ago the minister would preach fire and brimstone from the pulpit but not so now. I visited the inside of the Methodist chapel recently for the very first time and was surprised to find that what I had imagined would be grey austere and dark was none of those things, it is light with different shades of pink to the walls, light wood seating and altogether rather beautiful and welcoming. It is used for many different communal purposes as well as church services. The fact that Ron was a self-proclaimed atheist and enjoyed a good discussion on the subject of religion was to be calmed at all costs. He had already got himself into some heated discussions in the Old Inn. Miss Simmons was a small elderly spinster, always dressed in black, who lived in one of the old coastguard cottages behind Henscath. She kept herself to herself and lived with no electricity, using only oil lamps and a small kitchen range for cooking. She used the wash house across the yard to wash her clothes and there was no bathroom.   She waived away any offers the council made to modernise her house. Her only source of heating was from the fire in her living room.   Miss Simmons was a very strict and devout Methodist and walked to the village every Sunday morning to worship in the large Methodist chapel in the centre. On Sundays there was a black felt hat and black gloves added to the already black ensemble. Wendy and I found her quite scary and wondered if she might in fact be a witch as she never seemed to smile and had the most piercing old dark eyes. One Sunday morning Ron took it upon himself to clip back the hedges out in the lane, loudly whistling some obscure jazz number as he tended to do and as he got busy with the shears Miss Simmons appeared on her way to chapel. She stopped as she got level with him and tapped him on the shoulder with her stick causing him to wheel around suddenly in surprise.

"You've no business to be using any sort of blade on the Sabbath" she scolded him, to which Ron replied with something akin to "and you have no business to mind what other people do so mind your own" and he turned back to the work in hand, the whistling now louder than before. He had not bargained with the wrath he now received from the now puffing Miss Simmons as she let out a tirade of words and quotes from the bible that she clutched in her hands. Ron stood his ground and continued clipping the hedge telling her in no uncertain terms that he was as devoutly atheist as she was

Methodist and he would clip the hedge on any day he cared to. Miss Simmons stormed off down the lane, her tongue still lashing as she rounded the corner at the bottom as Ron feverishly continued clipping. Once she was out of sight he put down the shears and sought out my parents in the kitchen to tell them what had happened and how dare she. They told him in no uncertain terms to contain his temper and his views as it could have a major effect on their standing in the village.

It was unfortunate that Ron decided to treat the encounters with Miss Simmons as a game and the following Sunday at the same time, he again went into the lane to do more clipping, knowing that she would be coming by again and again Miss Simmons appeared. This time they were both ready for a fight and words flew like spitting fire. This time Miss Simmons had the last word, a quote from the Bible before turning and fiercely tap tapping with her stick away down the lane.

By the time Miss Simmons returned from chapel, Ron was in the kitchen making a cup of tea and recounting to my parents the heated discussion he had been having in the lane. This caused another heated discussion as my parents begged him to leave things alone and if it offended Miss

Simmons to see someone using a blade on a Sunday, then don't do it.

The following Sunday Ron was in the greenhouse planting seeds when he heard a noise behind him. Miss Simmons had come into the garden and was now standing in the doorway watching him.

"I hope that's not a knife you're using there Mr. Neville"

"It's a trowel and I'll thank you not to come into this garden and spy on me Miss Simmons" Ron retorted.

Miss Simmons removed her bible from her bag and began to quote once more about not using a blade on the Sabbath. It was almost as if she had actively sought him out for a heated discussion.

The arguments continued in the lane for weeks until one Sunday as the old lady began to speak, Ron turned on her and gave her a storm of words on his reasons for being atheist. Miss Simmons was of course horrified but stood her ground and the pair of them yelled at each other for the next ten minutes after which she suddenly bid him good day and walked quietly away. Ron was perplexed and not a little worried that he had taken things too far, after all she was just a little old lady, harmless other than her waspish tongue. The next Sunday he took his shears out to the lane, more out of curiosity than anything Sure enough along she came again and the shouting match was repeated on both sides, again she bid him a pleasant good day and carried on. At last he realised what was happening. Miss Simmons was actually enjoying the battle of words and the high volume debating. Perhaps for the first time in many years the lonely old lady felt someone was taking notice of her.

When Miss Simmons died a few years later, Ron was one of the first to arrive at the chapel for the funeral. It was the only funeral he ever attended in the village.

The summer season was now getting very much under way.   The cliffs and harbour swarming with people from the coaches for several hours and the cafes were kept busy providing ice creams and Cornish cream teas. This is not something that happens nowadays but back then when most people holidayed in this country and many people did not possess their own transport, coach trips were very much in vogue. By five o'clock the coaches departed and an almost eery silence pervaded the Cove for a while.   The guests at Henscath were for the most part pleasant and enjoyed their stay, my mother's cooking was a great success and my father took to the waiting, learning to balance several plates precariously in his hands and on his arms and , whilst his slightly acerbic Basil Fawlty type wit sometimes fell short for some of the guests, he could also be very charming which helped to counter some of his rather misplaced sarcasms.

One memorable family of four arrived one Saturday afternoon. Major Howlet, a large ruddy faced man, his small waif like wife and two pale teenage boys.

My mother showed the family to their rooms. The Major strutted around, opening cupboards, and wardrobes, looking out of the windows and generally making a barracks type inspection while his wife and the pale faced boys stood back. It seemed that he was unable to relax or detach himself from his military career.

Fortunately he found the rooms very 'adequate' and went to collect the cases from the car while his wife made apologetic noises about him to my mother.

Major Howlett was a stickler for timing. At ten to seven the gong was rung for dinner at seven and the family appeared scrubbed up and ready almost as the last bang on the gong sounded.

On the first evening all the guests had assembled in the dining room apart from one little lady holidaying on her own who appeared just after seven and was loudly tutted at by the Major.

"Good, good" he proclaimed as the first course arrived promptly "I like to see a well run ship" - an odd euphemism from an army man but it became a pet saying amongst the family for a few years after that. My father, unusually, managed to contain a caustic remark to the Major and the little lady who had arrived late, looked embarrassed and kept her eyes averted. As the week continued, the family arrived in the dining room just as punctually as the gong finished until one evening when my mother happened to glance out of the kitchen window just before dinner time and saw that the Major's car was not parked in the exact space he insisted on parking in every day, in fact it was not there at all.

The gong was duly rung at ten to seven but no Major or his family. Seven o'clock arrived and all the other guests were seated and they asked where the Major was. Dinner began and by half past seven, eight o'clock still no sign. My parents began to get quite concerned as a man like the Major would surely at least have phoned if they were not able to get back, but nothing at all had been heard from him.

Just after nine o'clock a car turned up the lane and reversed into the yard at the back of the house. It was the Major and his family. They emerged from the car, a sorry sight, damp, dishevelled and subdued. My parents went out to them to see if they were okay and the Major seemed unusually suppressed and slightly embarrassed but effusive with his apologies for their late arrival back.

It transpired that the family had hired a rowing boat on the Malpas estuary. The estuary is both tidal and known for its mudflats, a feeding ground for wildfowl and wading birds . They were warned about tide times and the Major admitted that his wife had mentioned the time on several occasions as they rowed along the creek but the Major had decided to carry on further up river until at last the tidal water deserted them and left them marooned in a sea of mud flats which would have swallowed them up if they had tried to step out of the boat. No mobile phones in those days and no one to see them, they had to wait six or seven hours for the tide to turn and come back to float them again and they had no food or water left by this time. It was probably lucky that a fine misty rain came down to soak them into the bargain, if the sun had been strong they would have been badly burned sitting out in the middle of the river with no shelter.

Their dinner was ruined by now and my mother provided them with hot drinks and rustled up some hot food for which they were very grateful.

The next night the gong was rung but the family did not appear until seven o clock and the booming voice of the Major was much quieter. It seemed that the experience of the day before had somehow pulled Major Howlet from his barrack room back into the normal world. The family were to return to Henscath for several more years.

The summer moved on, there was a big demand for pasties at the Old Inn and the guest intake was going well. Several of the guests would come year on year from now and become good friends of my parents. My father continued to wrestle and swear at the boiler and he and Ron produced a good crop of vegetables and salads from the garden. There were lawns to mow and roll with the big heavy iron roller.

The one problem that seemed to be getting worse was the rat and mouse population which could not be allowed to continue, quite apart from the fact that my mother's rodent phobia was and is the worst I have ever seen in anyone, she almost seemed to have an instinct that a mouse had gained access before anyone actually saw one. The rats were particularly partial to getting into the big jute sacks of potatoes outside the kitchen window for a feast and the mice had easy access to the house. The anthracite for the boiler was kept in a brick enclosure near the back door and on several occasions my father saw enormous king rats clambering about in there, although it was hard to know why they should have been attracted to anthracite, unless perhaps their nest was nearby.

Something had to be done and quickly. The council sent out their rodent control man who looked so much like a rat with long prominent front teeth, small black eyes and a rather strange gait, that it was hard to concentrate on the matter in hand. My parents were very much against the use of poison but the rat man insisted that there was no other way and proceeded to place the poisons in strategic places safely away from where other animals were likely to find it. He suggested my parents get a cat which might help in the future and with a couple of rat like twitches he left. Within a couple of weeks my father appeared home with the tiniest white kitten, a veritable ball of pure white fur, which he plucked from the pocket of his mac like a magician producing a white rabbit out of a hat.

My Father had already decided on a name for the kitten, though goodness knows where the idea came from. He was to be called Lucifer and at times over the years he certainly earned his title. I have to admit I thought for many years his name had to do with some connection between loose and fur! Ah the innocence of the young!

Although he started out so small, Lucifer grew and grew into an enormous white long haired cat, with one green eye and one blue. He was very handsome and very single minded, making it very clear that he was top of the pecking order both at home with us and to the rest of the cat population round about the Cove, in fact over the next year or so until Lucifer had to succumb to the knife to curtail his wander lust and fighting habits, he managed to sire many predominately white cats in the Cove. Bruno gave him a very wide birth from early on. Lucifer became an expert ratter and killed many a king rat as it tried to get into the potato sacks outside the kitchen window. As he matured Lucifer started wandering off for several days at a time, arriving home, usually with ears blackened with fleas and almost always with a war wound of some sort. Occasionally he would bring a present such as a dead rabbit or a rat or young pheasant, which he deposited on the back door step with some ceremony, the appreciation he looked for was not there and he would look quite disdainful whilst flicking his front paw at a lively black ear.

Lucifer's personality was odd. He usually slept on Wendy's or my bed and was very docile with us. He had crazy moments when he would skid up and down the corridor, ears flattened, completely mad. His favourite pastime however was to lie on the floor looking very gentle, inviting the innocent passer by to scratch his tummy. We learned very early on that this was just a trap, for as soon as hand touched tummy, it would be grabbed by all four legs and if you pulled your arm away there would be painful and deep gouges as he tried to hold on with all claws out. One macho house guest whose ability to complain was quite staggering, constantly banging on the kitchen door to complain about the strength of the morning tea, the birds squabbling in the chimneys above his bedroom or the placing of his table in the dining room, was not prepared to listen to my Mother's warnings to leave Lucifer well alone, especially as the one thing Lucifer did not seem to be able to control, was the tip of his tail which twitched incessantly, giving away the temper within.　Lucifer was lying on the midnight blue carpet in the lounge hall, looking like the cat in the Kosset carpet advertisement, watching my mother as she dusted a shelf, his tail twitching madly.　The macho man walked in.

"That's a fine cat you have there" he told my mother. "Good with animals I am".　My mother managed to refrain from suggesting that perhaps he should try a little harder with his fellow human beings. He bent towards Lucifer who was now twitching his tail quite violently.

"Oh I really wouldn't touch him at the moment" my mother warned.　"He is a bit prone to sudden temper and you could get badly scratched".

"Oh no I'll be fine" the man continued "I have a way with animals, you'll see"

"No really" my mother insisted " I really would leave him alone at the moment."
The man ignored the advice and plunged his hand onto Lucifer's tummy.

"There, see I told you they all love me" he said as Lucifer began to purr loudly.　He ruffled the fur a bit more until the cat, ears flat on his head and tail whisking a storm, grabbed the man's naked forearm with all of his large claws.　The man withdrew his hand quickly but the cat held on shredding the skin on his arm, blood poured from the deep wounds.

"You should warn people about that animal" he shouted "It needs putting down." He turned away and stormed upstairs to his room.

There were three buses a day which served our cove. Big green double decker Western National buses which looked very incongruous snaking slowly round the bends on the steep narrow road past our house and on another five hundred yards to the very edge of the cliff outside the hotel with just enough room to turn round before stopping for passengers. To anyone who happened to be sitting innocently at the front of the top deck for the first time, as many holiday makers did, there was a moment when it looked for all the world as if you were going straight over the cliff and on several occasions there were yells as unsuspecting Grockles feared for their lives. The bus would wait outside the hotel for half an hour or so before heading back towards the Lizard and Helston. This gave the conductor and driver time for a quick pint in the hotel bar.

There was a call one morning from a house at the Lizard, some five miles away. The bus conductor had discovered Lucifer in the luggage compartment under the stairs as they arrived in Lizard village and borrowed the phone in a local house to let my parents know. Unfortunately the travelling cat had leapt off the bus before the conductor could catch him. He said he would keep an eye out for him when he returned to the Lizard in the afternoon before his third and last scheduled visit to the cove.

Another phone call several hours later and my parents were asked to come and meet the four thirty bus.

The bus crawled back up the hill and stopped at the bottom of our garden. The conductor showed my astounded Father, the cat, once more reclining in the luggage compartment. Apparently when the bus made its second visit to the Lizard, Lucifer was there at the bus stop and just got back on like any other passenger. He did this several more times over the years and never once missed the last bus home.

Lucifer had his own way of dealing with unwanted animal visitors. My mother had taken charge of a pretty golden cocker spaniel whilst their owners were away. Sherry as he was called was quite elderly and spent most of the time asleep and really was no physical problem for Lucifer but nevertheless he took a dislike to the dog and would sit in wait for him every morning on the corner of the kitchen table. As Sherry wandered slowly into the kitchen for his breakfast, passing the table on the way, Lucifer took a hard and calculated swipe at his long pelt like ear, causing Sherry to yelp loudly looking very surprised. This became a daily routine, the cat always remembering, the dog always surprised having forgotten. Lucifer lived to a ripe old age. He was arthritic and not too well by the time my parents decided to move to Surrey many years later so my mother took the painful choice of euthanasia for him before we made the move to Surrey.

Lucifer in his twilight years

*Q and Betty, my parents, early 1940's
Falmouth, taken by street photographer*

*Ron and Q on a walking trip in Cornwall - 1930's
(looking like a pair of POW's!)*

Betty and Q with Wendy 1946
Kynance Cove

Wendy and Penny on front terrace at Henscath
1948

Chapter FIVE

Henscath School Husbandry and Grandparents
1948-1950

Henscath School officially opened for the beginning of September term 1949. My father's class was fairly sparse at first with about six or seven pupils whose ages varied from six to eight years old. For my mother in the little class room at the other end of the house there were a few more including Wendy, the majority of the children being between three and four years old. It was an exciting day, the parents arriving with their children in time for the 10.00 am start. My parents greeted them all and showed the children where to hang their outdoor clothes and bags and put on their indoor shoes. All the children had on their new uniforms and for the first day, the children were accompanied to their class rooms by their parents.

School began at ten o clock with lunch for the school children at 12.30. The little ones aged three to five years were either collected by their parents or taken up to the hotel car park to wait for the bus at two-o-clock. The bus conductor would then take charge of the children and parents would be waiting for their small offspring at various points on the way back to the village. How precarious that seems now but there were no casualties. The older children were collected an hour later.

My mother had studied various reading methods and decided to use the Old Lob books and flash cards which proved to be very successful. The books were well illustrated and the children could connect with the Farmer, Old Lob and the animals on his farm. I remember the books very well and can remember every page of the first one.

Old Lob was a farmer whose animals consisted of Mr Dan the sheep dog, Miss Tibbs the tabby cat, Master Willy the pig and Mr. Grumps the goat (Mr Grumps says NO!!) I loved Mr. Grumps but was also slightly scared of him. There was Mother hen and her chicks which included Percy the bad chick, "I am Percy the bad chick" he announced to the reader. I loved Percy. Finally there was Mrs Cuddy the cow and Dobbin the cart horse. The books were all about life on the farm with Old Lob. The last book in the series was entitled The Move which worried me quite a lot as I didn't like the idea of them moving to another farm. It has only occurred to me now whilst writing about

Old Lob, that there was never a mention of Mrs Lob, perhaps Old Lob was a bachelor. The books were accompanied by flash cards, large reading cards containing some of the words we had seen in the books.

My mother was incredibly proficient at teaching small children, it seemed she had a natural gift for it and all the children in her small classes were reading fluently by the age of five or six. She could be very strict but was also very kind and the children thrived under her direction.

For play time the large front lawn was designated for the older children and the small lawn for the younger ones where they could be kept an eye on from the house.

Practically all of the pupils lived in the local area, either in the village or in the Cove, several came from families connected with the local Naval Air base at Culdrose but who lived nearby.

I do not remember there ever being a problem with Wendy and me being daughters of the teachers, we were treated exactly the same as any other pupil just with the added advantage of being able to walk up the corridor to the classroom in the mornings. I remember longing to join in at the school and to go on the bus like some of the children although I was later to change my mind when I had to walk a mile and a half to catch the school bus to Helston Grammar school with another long steep walk in front of me at the other end.

A problem presented itself. From the cloakroom the youngest children had to walk the length of the house to get to their classroom. This entailed walking the long narrow corridors which had been freshly painted white. Grubby little hands inevitably touched the walls as they went to and from their classroom and quickly the walls became stained and greasy. Out came the distemper again and the stains were covered up on several occasions until my Mother came up with an inspirational idea. She told the children that they would all have to carry a big clay pot full of water on their heads every time they went up or down the corridor. This of course was imaginary play but the children all took it very seriously. They walked in single file whilst imagining the clay pot balanced precariously on their heads holding them on with both hands to avoid spilling an imaginary drop of water.

Happy children, clean walls.

The school thrived and its reputation grew. Occasionally there were difficulties and worries with some of the pupils. One little girl Catherine, just didn't seem to get the hang of writing. She could read quite well but her writing made no sense. She was an intelligent happy child which did not seem to fit with this inability to grasp the written word. Then one day my mother realised to her amazement what was happening. She took a piece of her writing to my father and asked him to read it. He couldn't, it didn't make any sense and then my Mother held a mirror over it and there it was, Catherine was doing mirror writing, in the reflection of the mirror her writing and spelling were perfect.

Sammy was five years old when he arrived at the school. He lived on a small isolated farm up on the moors. He was a tiny pale chap, blond hair and painfully thin. My Mother greeted him warmly and showed him where to hang his coat and leave his outdoor shoes. Sammy was a bit of a worry from the start. He was shy and in the isolation of his farm up on the moors, hadn't really played or mixed with other children. He was slow to learn and rarely smiled or spoke.

By morning break time the quarter bottles of full cream milk had been delivered in metal crates by the tallest man I have ever seen, who went by the name of Tiny. The children sat at their desks drinking out of the bottles through waxed paper straws

and were each given a morning biscuit.
Sammy didn't touch his. Lunch time came
on that first day and all the children
tucked into their meals except for Sammy
who didn't even lift his fork. My Mother
tried to encourage him but to no avail, he
ate nothing, he drank nothing.

When it was time to go home and
Sammy's mother came to collect him, my
Mother took her to one side.

"I'm sorry" my Mother said "but Sammy
has had nothing to eat at all, he wouldn't
touch his morning biscuit and milk or his
lunch."

"Oh don't you worry about that" Sammy's
mother retorted, "he always has a good
hot dinner in the evening".

"Well what sort of thing does he like?" my
mother asked.

"He always has a nice hot boiled egg for
his dinner" was the answer.

My parents continued to be very
concerned about the waif like child and
tried various ways to get him to eat but it
seemed a hopeless task.

Eventually in exasperation, my Father
came up with a new idea, they would sit
Sammy at a table in the cloakroom on his
own to eat his lunch, perhaps eating by
himself would do it. Sammy was duly
taken to the cloakroom at lunch time and
left alone with his lunch in front of him.

When my parents came back, they were amazed and delighted to find Sammy had finished every scrap on his plate. They tried it again the next day and again all eaten. They were so pleased and gave Sammy lots of praise. The next day he rejoined the other children again for lunch but once again disappointingly wouldn't touch his meal. This was odd behaviour but they didn't feel they could keep leaving him on his own in the cloakroom to eat.

The weekend came and my Father got ready for some gardening. He went into the cloakroom to put on his wellingtons, a few seconds later, a yell followed by some expletives. My Mother ran in to see what had happened. My Father had put his foot into a pile of spaghetti bolognaise in one wellington and in the other boot lay mince and onions. A lesson never to underestimate a five year old.

Sammy did in fact thrive and eventually took over the farm from his parents.

Each Friday afternoon my Father would read to the children for an hour from such children's classics as Treasure Island, Coral Island, Lorna Doone and the Three Musketeers. He managed to get through quite a number of these books. We all loved the reading hour and I am sure it was what spurred most of us on to read books for ourselves and versed us in knowing many of the classics that we may not have got around to reading.

My father's classroom was divided into two sections. There was the group of five to eight year olds on one side of the room and the group of eight to eleven year olds on the other. The mix in one room worked surprisingly well, a certain amount of integration but also a division when required. During the ten years or so that the school ran, only one child failed to pass their eleven plus exam.

I remember so well when my turn came to take the eleven plus in the January of 1958. There were three of us in the lounge where it would be suitably quiet. Three tables in the middle of the room upon each of which were two brand new sharpened pencils with rubbers on top and a ruler and the exam papers turned over so they could not be read until the exam actually started. Old Mrs. George, an ex head teacher, presided over the exam as invigilator, a large comforting mother hen-like figure with her white hair tied into an untidy bun at the back of her head, sitting in the comfy armchair by a roaring fire. We turned the papers over at the appointed time. I remember that many of the questions involved diagrams where you had to work out which way to turn a certain shape so that it would fit with the others or which one was the odd one out or match up pairs of shapes. There were comprehension questions and arithmetic questions and a section headed General Intelligence which contained lists of questions such as rearrange these sentences like – Jane like a bird flew. Another list was: one word in each group of four means the same or nearly the same as the word in capitals, write this word down.

a) CUT: knife sever canal wound
b) TWIN: engine triplet brother duplicate
It felt at the time as if there was a whole book to get through, pages of word or graphic puzzles and arithmetic, in the time allowed for the exam.

At last time was up, signalled by Mrs. George ringing a small brass bell although I'm not sure why as she was only sitting a couple of feet from us
and could just as easily have told us. Now we would have to wait a long time before we knew if we had passed the exam.

There were radio programmes designed for schools which proved very popular and successful. For the older children, 'Singing together' and 'Rhythm and Melody' which as their titles suggest, were designed to teach the children to sing and gain an appreciation for music. A deep voiced male presented Singing together where we learned to sing such ballads as 'the Ash Grove' the 'Sky Boat song' and 'Cockles and Mussels' which we joined in with and sung with gusto from the words on the pamphlet.

Rhythm and Melody was perhaps a little more technical and explained a little about musical notes and staves but there were a few songs to be sung as well such as the rousing 'Kije' 'Kije was a soldier bold, a soldier bold was he, he fought so bravely for the Czar, the pride of the cavalry' which we all loved.

For the smaller children there was Music and Movement. This took place in the lounge hall in the centre of the house where there was plenty of room to dance and skip about to the nursery rhymes and the instructions to pretend to be a chicken or a lion or a bud opening into a beautiful flower or whatever the Presenter suggested they should try to be.

That first term at Henscath proved to be a great success and school reports were sent out at the end of the Christmas term with very favourable comments received back from parents.

1950 was the first full year of school, pasty making, anemone growing and the guest season. By March my father had once again decided to add another string to their bow. He had been debating for some time, the possibility of keeping pigs and made the decision that now would be the time to start.

Knowing absolutely nothing about such things he sought advice from his nearest neighbour at Trenance farm.

George Pascoe was the seventh generation of a family who had been farming his land for a hundred or so years. He was thick set and had a ruddy face that told of his many hours in all weathers and his hard work gave the family a comfortable living from his few stony acres both with livestock and crops. His wife Mary took in bed and breakfast visitors. Their grey granite farmhouse was immaculate, the front garden a picture of flowers from spring to autumn.

George kept pigs and cattle and the pigs were usually to be found snuffling around in the field just outside the farmyard (now a chocolate factory). The farmyard was a large square of cracked concrete surrounded by outbuildings, workshops milking parlour and stabling for the cart horse. Chickens ran free and roosted in the barns at night. The farmyard was always busy and smelled of dung and straw.

George gave my father much valuable

advice on what type of pigs he should keep, on the husbandry of swine and what type of sties to build for them. Much advice was also given at various times by farmers he met in the pub but he stuck with the advice George gave.

With no previous handyman skills at all, my father and Ron proceeded to build two magnificent sties with their own enclosed yards at the top of the back garden. They were so sturdily built that they could probably have withstood a bomb blast. The next thing was to go and purchase the pigs at Helston livestock market and George went with them to help choose carefully. They decided on two Large Whites, a male and a female which were transported home and herded up the garden into the largest of the two sties. The pigs settled well into their new environment and produced several drifts of piglets in their time. I was fascinated by these animals and grew to love them. I could get my arm through the wire fencing just enough to tickle the boar behind his ears which he loved, he would then go into raptures sculling about on his back, feet in the air. I even grew to like the awful smell of them and would join my father in taking the pig swill to them each evening. Soon after the arrival of the pigs, a large chicken house arrived on a lorry and my father then proceeded to build an enormous chicken wire enclosure around it. We heard the rumble of George's old van coming up the lane one day and he had brought a box of yellow chicks, all cheeping merrily inside. "You'll need to keep they warm fer a bit longer" he advised my father in his deep growly voice. "I've brought you a bag of the special feed they'll need to 'ave until they're a bit stronger," he turned to Wendy and me standing there excitedly, he ruffled the tops of our heads, we loved George, he always took notice of us and made good jokes. "Orright are ee?" he asked us more as a statement than a question. "You gonna help yor Dad with they?" We certainly were, we had only seen chicks in story books and now here was the real thing. The chicks were transferred into a small cage in the scullery and Wendy and I helped to feed them and give them some water.

The next morning, we raced into the scullery to see how they had fared overnight and found to our horror that every one of them was dead. We were horrified and burst into tears. My mother came to calm us and called my father when she saw the cluster of little stiff chicks. Then the horrible truth was revealed. My father had put the sack of chick feed on the floor next to a similar type bag of fertiliser and he had given the chicks fertiliser by mistake. The chicks were duly buried and tears dried. A week or so later George arrived with another clutch of chicks and gave my father a jovial dressing down. "They'll need chick feed" he said "fertiliser will never make 'em grow." He gave Wendy and me a big pantomime wink. The chickens grew and thrived in their roomy surroundings.

Soon the sow became pregnant and produced nine healthy piglets. The sow and her offspring were transferred to the adjacent sty just in case the clumsy father of nine should lie on them by mistake. Wendy and I loved the piglets and spent hours watching them and stroking them when we could. The pigs grew but came the day when they were taken away. Wendy and I had no idea where or why they had to go. I stood back against the pebble dash wall of the house, tears running down my cheeks as they were herded into a lorry. The smallest one ran by me and bit my little finger in passing. I would not correlate the delicious pork chops and roasts we had soon after, with the passing of the pigs.

Although Ron's contribution to the running of the guest house was to do the washing up and help where beds and furniture needed changing around to accommodate different guests, he was still very keen to help out with the cooking, so it was decided that he should cook breakfast for Wendy and me as he assured my mother that although his cooking skills had proved dubious to say the least so far, he was quite capable of putting together a little breakfast for two children. Certainly his breakfasts were memorable and stayed with both my sister and me, never to be forgotten. There were four choices in his repertoire. The first and most frequent offering being porridge. This thick glutinous grey glue like mess had the extra surprise of large inedible lumps, it was then swamped in full cream milk and topped with golden syrup. Another dish was charcoaled black toast given a cursory scrape in the sink, with either rock hard or virtually raw fried egg on top and accompanied by crispy black bacon which fell to dust on being touched by a fork. Then there was a dish called bubble and squeak which bore no resemblance to that particular dish, grey/green, lumpy and invariably cold by the time it reached the table. At the weekends Ron would often cook kippers for the whole family and manage not to burn them. However they were so full of bones as to render them almost completely inedible. Ron's piece de resistance however and which he would also cook for himself to eat whilst reading in bed at night, was a whole Spanish onion with cloves stuck into it and boiled in milk for what seemed like several days, this at least was edible and never burnt but oddly I have never felt the need to try it out again since I have been doing my own cooking! Ron was obviously well ahead of his time when it came to deconstructing a dish although his efforts varied slightly from the meaning we now give to that word in the preparing of meals.

Ron had recovered to some degree from his tragic loss but he still found the need to spend much time on his own and so whenever he had the chance, he would set out across the moors often with Bruno in tow. He climbed down hazardous cliffs into small coves discovering hidden caves and encountering families of seals and other sea life. He collected rocks and stones, studying their composition and age. The landing at the top of the back stairs in Henscath became filled with rock samples he was studying. He spent much time at one of the family's favourite visiting spots, a small cove called Poltesco, or Carleon cove a little further up the coast from Cadgwith and close to the village of Ruan Minor. Poltesco is a hidden gem attained from inland by a very narrow single track road to a car park, now National Trust owned, from where you can walk through shady woods and glades past gurgling water finding its way down to a large pool and the sea. From the dark and cool of the woods you come quite suddenly out into the sunlight where you find the pool and to your left the remains of what was once a very large building and two derelict buildings still standing, one of the buildings is circular and was a capstan house in years gone by when Poltesco cove was used for the pilchard fishing industry. Here too once stood a major Victorian serpentine factory using the pool as its leat. Now there are toads to be seen around the edges of the water and brown trout leap. But for all this eye catching history, the main thing that catches the eye is not the buildings or the water or the cliffs but the beach itself. There is no sand here other than at a very low tide. The whole cove is covered in colourful rocks and boulders. The majority of the boulders are formed of pink granite, then there is banded gneiss and red and green serpentine.

This was a place of wonder for Ron as a rock collector and Poltesco had a unique quality of calm. There would have been very few people visiting it in the forties and even now there are rarely more than a handful of people to be found there at any time of the year.

1950 progressed with the summer term being the busiest of all times. The days' timetable began with, up at six, make a couple of dozen pasties and lunches for the school children, then breakfast for the guests followed by bed making and cleaning. The school children arrived to begin their day at ten. My mother leading the smallest children to their classroom, all carrying their pretend pots on their heads. Now it was time for Uncle Ron to take charge of me, taking me out for walks in the pushchair or playing games or making up stories about his rock collection and his hazardous adventures looking for them.

I suppose one of the reasons that our Uncle Ron was so loved by us was that he was the only other 'family' that we had even if he wasn't real family, he certainly seemed like it. We didn't know our Grandparents very well at all. They did come to visit once a year or two years and so it was difficult to become close to them. How different they were from each other. On the one hand Granny and Grandad who were our father's mother and step-father (my real Grandad died in his thirties as a result of an appendix operation). Granny remarried Percy, a gentle man who had suffered shell shock in the war which had slightly distorted his face. Granny Hodge was little with grey curly hair and thin rimmed spectacles. She looked old to us and a bit old fashioned and wore furry plaid slippers with a pom on top but she was very kind and we liked it when she came to stay. We would all go into Helston on the bus and she would buy us new toys although we knew she didn't have much money.

Frances Kearney, our mother's mother was altogether a different kettle of fish. I only remember one visit when she was with my grandfather Jack because he died from leukaemia when I was very young. I remember sitting on my grandfather's knee in the kitchen while he did some magic tricks, like appearing to pull the top of his thumb off and move it up and down behind his hand. He stuck bits of cigarette paper on the ends of his fingers to do the 'two little dicky birds sitting on a wall' trick. The relationship between my rather eccentric fiery redheaded Irish grandfather and my quick tempered beautiful grandmother was to say the least stormy but they stayed together because they needed each other in their lives. My grandfather made a real imprint on my mind during that one short visit and I have never forgotten him. Frances wore rather short skirts, dark sheer stockings and fashionable high heeled shoes, not very appropriate for our local terrain. She wore a black fur coat, had lots of curly black hair and wore dark blue tinted glasses, she looked like a film star to me and I was a little in awe of her. She gave me my first proper pop single 'Will you love me Tomorrow' by the Shirelles. I was amazed that my Grandmother could know about such things as pop records. She had been a concert pianist in her early twenties but was pushed so hard that she had a nervous breakdown and never touched a piano again. She was something of an artist too. Her voice was an odd mixture of cultured Dublin and London and really fascinated me. She drank black tea into which she spooned condensed milk and she smoked constantly with a short black and gold cigarette holder.

Wendy and I were always on our best behaviour when our Grandparents came to visit and they didn't really feel like proper family although we knew they were. The rather 'colourful' marriage of Jack and Frances was probably not helped by the fact that Jack was in the merchant navy and away for long periods at the start of their marriage. When he came out of the navy he tried his hand at many different crafts and was also an inventor, the only invention I heard of was the Kearney cutter, a bread cutting machine which was manufactured and sold. He also started a small toy making factory which produced pedal cars, rocking horses, dolls prams and dolls houses. Wendy had one of his red metal pedal cars which sadly rusted away eventually and a small green pram which I think was made from wood. Jack was a teller of ghost stories and a man of great imagination. His earnings dipped and rose through the years which meant many a change of residence and area in London. Sometimes they lived in the Kensington area and sometimes it was the Elephant and Castle. I doubt they were ever bored.

CHAPTER SIX

Christmas and Polio
1950 – 1952

By the end of 1950, my parents were feeling some considerable relief as their hard work showed them to be in profit for the first time. With the Autumn term finished it was time to turn their attention to preparations for Christmas.

Christmas at Henscath was a wonderful time. The Christmas holidays were the only time during the year when the family could properly relax and spend whole days together and my parents certainly embraced the Christmas season. In the fifties there were no packs of mince pies to buy or mincemeat to put in them for that matter. No ready made Christmas cake to take off the shelf. Everything had to be made at home so there was a constant smell of wonderful things being baked, hand raised pork pies, Christmas puddings, sponges for trifles, mince pies, Christmas cake, eclairs and the list went on. From September when the last of the guests had gone we lived entirely in the downstairs section of the house and for Christmas every part of it was covered in decorations. It was the custom then to have swathes of paper streamers on the ceilings. My father took this to some extreme using rolls and rolls of wide stretchy crepe streamers of every bright garish colour to criss cross all over the ceilings in the hall and corridors and the lounge and dining room until they were completely covered. The Christmas tree was chosen carefully so that it just touched the ceiling in the centre of the large square bay window in the lounge. It must often have rained on Christmas day because my memories of the Christmas tree include two galvanised buckets, one on each side to catch the drips of rain as it came through the ceiling. We decorated the tree with glass and fragile thin metal tree ornaments after which there were swathes of tinsel and on the top a rosebud doll took pride of place as the fairy I still have her although her arms have come off and she has a permanent wink as one eye is stuck shut. I don't remember there being any Christmas tree lights but I remember Wendy and I sitting cross legged on the floor looking up at the tree in awe when it was finished as children always did and always do.

On Christmas eve Wendy and I put pillow cases for stockings at the end of our beds and lay half hoping we would and half hoping we wouldn't spy Santa creeping out of the fireplace in our bedroom with his sack.

In the morning the sacks were full to the brim with dolls, new clothes, sweets and all sorts of toys plus an orange and nuts. I think the fullness of the sacks was because it was only at Christmas and on birthdays that we got any special gifts whereas now I notice with the young children in the family that they have little presents and clothes bought for them throughout the year. Comparatively, clothes especially were very expensive then and we had few so they had to last and as was the custom most of mine were hand me downs including scratchy vests and liberty bodices.

Two stocking presents stand out in my mind. We each got a small plastic black box which appeared to have no opening. It was a long while before Wendy found a tiny concealed lever which when pressed released a long spring of the type you have inside a biro with a little red smiley face inserted on the end, a mini Jack in a box.

The other is a memory for more obvious reasons. Wendy woke in the early hours and discovered Father Christmas had been. She woke me up to tell me the good news and we set about opening our presents straight away. Amongst the presents were two plastic trumpets one blue, one white and of course we just had to try them out. My father arrived bleary eyed in the bedroom. "Come on girls save the presents for the morning and do not blow on your trumpets". The temptation was too great and after he had gone back to bed we tried to blow them ever so quietly. Back he came a little more impatient this time. The third time he came in we were given a warning. "If you blow your trumpets any more tonight it will be smacked bottoms" This didn't trouble us particularly because my parents firmly did not believe in corporal punishment and had never smacked us in our lives. A couple of words from my father were plenty to make us behave. However we just had to have one more go. My father marched into the room told us to lie on our tummies, walked up between the beds and pulled back the covers. Thwack came his hands one on each quivering winceyette clad bottom before he pulled up the covers again and retired from the room in silence. It was the only time we were ever smacked and we certainly didn't do it again.

On Christmas morning after a breakfast of fresh grapefruit and boiled eggs followed by the opening of presents round the tree, we went to church in the village, my mother who was completely tone deaf and

Wendy who appeared to have inherited the trait, sang lustily. Then it was across the road and into the Old Inn for a glass of punch and home for lunch. The 'punch' as it was called was made by David throughout the year by putting the last small drop of any bottle of any alcohol into a bowl. By Christmas the 'punch' with a few additions of fruit juices and fruit, was ready. The alcoholic content must have been through the roof but it was always well received and must have brought quite a glow to those who dared to try it. In fact David was well known for his practical jokes from behind the bar. Sometimes he would get hold of a great green grasshopper, rarely seen these days, and place it on the bar in front of a customer who was becoming very inebriated. The customer would think he or she was hallucinating and beat a retreat from the bar. Another of David's jokes was to place bits of money on a hot plate behind the bar and then put it on the bar for a customer to pick up as his change, this also caused more than a little consternation.

Plenty of friends and neighbours came to the house for drinks and food over the Christmas period but after the visit to church on Christmas morning it was always just the four of us for Christmas

day and Boxing day and it felt incredibly special. Oddly I do not remember Ron being there for Christmas and I have no idea where he must have gone, one of those questions I didn't think to ask when I got older before it was too late.
Once back from church Wendy and I would play with our new toys while my father lit a fire in the lounge and arranged the settee and armchairs around it while my mother prepared the cold lunch of hand raised pork pie, pates, bread and salad followed by trifle, eclairs meringues and mince pies which were eaten sitting cosily around the fire place. By the time we had finished lunch it was time to switch the radio on and listen to the Queen's speech. We played board games, then at six o clock it was time to go and put on our best clothes for Christmas dinner in the dining room. The table was covered in a white damask table cloth and adorned with beautiful arrangements of greenery and crackers. Dressing up in our best made it all seem very special and grown up. The electric fires were on at either end of the room to brighten things up and keep us warm. I have often wondered whether people generally had the propensity to eat greater amounts of food than we do now. None of us were overweight – well perhaps me a bit with

what they told me was puppy fat - but on Christmas day having had the eggs toast and grapefruit for breakfast, and the large cold lunch plus a piece of Christmas cake at tea time, this was then followed by a large Christmas dinner of chicken with all the normal accoutrements we have today, finished off with Christmas pudding and Cornish clotted cream and more trifle. Wonderful fare but so much of it.

On Boxing Day there was the annual meeting of the Cury Hunt outside the Old Inn. This of course being in the 1950's there were no anti hunt demonstrations, it was just a part of local tradition and if anyone had anti views about it they kept them to themselves. The Masters of the hunt and hounds sat on fine huge strong horses, the Master of the hunt in a bright red jacket and the Master of the hounds in a green jacket, they wore immaculate white ruffled shirts underneath. The foxhounds bayed excitedly but kept close to the Master of the Hunt and the horses. Drink flowed in silver chalices and home made pies and fancies were handed up to the huntsmen. The supporting group of hunt chasers young and old turned up dressed in black jackets and riding jackets on a motley assortment of horses and ponies.

Quite a large crowd supported the hunt

each year and once they were ready, the Hunt Master blew the familiar notes of the hunting horn, leading off up the road at a trot with all the hounds following behind. It was quite a sight and seemed very far removed from the fact that they were off in such numbers and finery to find a fox to kill.

That Christmas was a particularly happy and relaxing time and so no one could have prepared the family for the events that were to follow in the year of 1951. There had been a National outbreak of polio since the end of the war and now it was beginning to invade Cornwall. There were a few cases locally, a very worrying time for everyone. My mother began to feel ill in late spring of that year and was diagnosed with the horrendous crippling paralysing disease that polio is. She was to spend the next six months fighting for her life often in an iron lung. The isolation was total so there was no visiting from her family to give encouragement and love.

It was very sudden for two young children to have their mother taken away and not really understand what was going on, especially as we were not allowed to see her at all and six months is a very long time in a young child's life. Wendy now aged six, had a slightly better understanding than me and even at such a young age tried to console me and look after me.

Of course I don't remember too much about it but I have my own slightly blurred memories of that time.

A big ambulance negotiated the rough lane and took our mother away on a stretcher. My father following in the shooting brake to the Truro isolation hospital, twenty five miles away. We knew something very serious and scary was happening. Uncle Ron looked after us until my father returned, he must have been absolutely devastated at having to leave her in that, at the time, dreadful hospital with its sombre grey stone face; a reminder of the days when it had been a workhouse. The nursing staff were starchy and officious for the most part as was the custom then for whatever reason. I remember odd little cameos of that time like watching Wendy, standing on the stone floor of the kitchen, patiently waiting for my father and uncle Ron to attempt yet again, to put her hair into acceptable plaits for school. They ended up wonky as usual but a little better with practice over the months.

Mrs. Bishop from the Coastguard houses behind Henscath helped to look after us children. She was very kind and mopped up a lot of the tears we shed over that time.

Of course both the school and the summer visitor intake came to a halt that year. The school children had to be found different schools to attend, some permanently and some who would come back to Henscath in time, to continue their education there. My father decided to carry on teaching Wendy at home until such time as the school might re-open. My father and Ron carried on with the anemone growing and made an attempt to carry on with the pasty making for the Old Inn. Ron took charge of preparing the vegetables while my father attempted to make the pastry. He rolled it out and cut the rounds with the same saucepan lid that my mother always used but by the time he was ready to add the filling, the rounds of pastry had shrunk to half their size, it was as if they were elasticated. He tried to make the pastry several more times but each time he tried to roll it and cut out the rounds, the same thing happened.

Eventually he decided to tackle the problem from a different direction. He rolled the pastry out as thinly as possible and took an enormous saucepan lid to cut out huge rounds. He then waited until they shrank to the required size before adding the meat and vegetables. I would imagine the taste of the over worked pastry left a great deal to be desired.

I cannot know nor do I remember how those six months passed at Henscath, nor how my father and my mother managed emotionally through that time of waiting and waiting to know if my mother would survive and return to us. I do not know how my father and uncle Ron got by with no income from either the school or the guests and I don't remember that time ever being talked about.

All I remember is that on one day strange people came to the house with equipment which was set up in my parents bedroom and a brand new bed arrived. I remember sensing a strange atmosphere and everyone rushing around looking very serious. Mrs. Bishop came to clean the house and kept telling Wendy and me to "get out from under her feet" and then hugging us a lot.

My father sat us down in the kitchen next to the old tortoise boiler and told us that our Mummy was coming home this very afternoon and we were to be good girls and keep very quiet, no sudden noises. We were bursting with joy and practised creeping up and down the hall. Mrs. Bishop came and gave Wendy and me what she called "a good wash and brush up." My teddy's head had come off yet again, despite Ron's efforts at sewing it back and Mrs. Bishop sewed it on properly for me. She gave us both a lovely cuddle and told us that we must be "good girls and be very quiet". So we were glad we had practised the creeping up the hall. We waited and waited and at last the ambulance reversed in through the gate and brought our mother home again.

A starchy nurse climbed out of the ambulance as we were about to run up to it and told us, "You will be able to see your mother as soon as we have made her comfortable, now off you go and play" It was so hard to go off but we had no choice.

An age later we heard the starchy nurse and our father calling us. They found us playing in the big heap of old ashes from the boiler piled up at the side of the house, we were covered from head to foot in ash. The nurse tut tutted. They brushed us off as well as possible and took us to see our mother . Again I do not remember our first sight of her after all that time but I am told that I stood by the bed, hand in hand with Wendy and because my three year old mind thought she had just gone off and left us, my first words to her were

"I don't like you."

My mother was told emphatically that she

would never walk again but whoever it was told her that had not reckoned with my mother's will power, also there were some new and revolutionary ideas on how to care for affected muscle wasted limbs. Gone were the splints and constricting leg braces which were attached to weak limbs to try and straighten them, instead the weak and fragile limbs were worked on and exercised in order to re-stimulate the muscles as far as possible. My mother had extensive physiotherapy over months until came the great day when she began to walk, first with crutches and eventually on her own. She made an incredible recovery much to the amazement of the medical profession.

Sadly the one total memory I have of those times was the first time my mother attempted to walk the length of the house down the narrow corridors. Wendy and I were at the other end of the house watching this momentous occasion but one of us had left a small dolls pram in the corridor which somehow got overlooked and my mother fell over it before our eyes. All those years ago but I can picture it like a slow motion film even now. She broke her fragile leg and the ambulance came again to take her to the hospital. I thought she was going away for a long long time again and apparently was inconsolable.

In fact it was only a few days before she returned with her leg in plaster and another whole healing process had to begin again and with grit and determination she recovered in the most incredible way and the following year took up the guest house, school and pasty making once more. There was no such thing as counselling in those days and I venture to say that it wasn't needed anyway. Of course it was a terrible time in the family but with the love of family and the friends around us we got through it in our own ways.

CHAPTER SEVEN

The Coronation and the Six Queens
1952-1953

In February 1952 came the news that King George VI had died. The young twenty five year old Elizabeth would accede the throne and her coronation at Westminster Abbey was set for June 1953.

There was much discussion in the village as to planning the celebration of this event and much focus on entertainments for the children. With nearly a year to prepare, grand decisions were made for a huge party to be held in the cricket field. Mullion has always held a carnival day so it was decided that the Coronation year carnival would outstrip all the carnivals that had gone before.

Joan Truscott came up with a wonderful idea for a float to be entitled the Six Queens of England and the costumes would be as near to authentic as it was possible to be. The six Queens would be Joan's daughter Susan as the newly crowned Queen Elizabeth II. Wendy was to be Queen Elizabeth I, I would be Queen Victoria, Jane and Marianne who were sisters living in the caravan field and who Wendy and I were firm friends with, Jane being Wendy's age and Marianne my age,

would become Queen Mary I, and Queen Ann. Another friend from the village, Maria, was to be Queen Mary II.
Work started straight away on the costumes, our mothers getting together to discuss, design and choose materials, the fathers getting involved too with the making of crowns and sceptres etc. and in my father's case, painting heraldry signs on the white crinoline dress for Queen Elizabeth I, an outer green coat dress worn over the crinoline like an open coat. Once all the designs were agreed and material bought, the mothers all got together with their sewing machines, cups of tea and cigarettes and thus began the making of the most fabulous and ornate costumes for us six queens. There were a lot of fittings to be done and we all dreaded having to go and stand still for ages to be measured or have sleeves and bodices fitted. The grandest dresses were certainly the two Elizabeths with all their finery. Elizabeth I in her sage green and the painted inner dress with pearls in her ornate head gear and Elizabeth II in a deep purple velvet robe with an 'ermine' trim along with the Coronation crown and sceptre. Mary Queen of Scots wore black with a tall head dress and much white lace and ruffles. Queen Mary II ornate and with colour to her costume. Queen Anne

131

and Queen Victoria played by Marianne and me, both five years old at the time were the least ornate. Marianne in quite a frumpy dull green/grey dress and fairly nondescript crown, authentically correct and me as Queen Victoria, obviously after the demise of Prince Albert, as I was dressed in black with just a small white lace trim. I had the star of the garter blue sash around me and a small silver coronet. However I thought I was the bees knees in this outfit and there is a photo of me on the day of the carnival with the dress lifted right up to my knickers in order not to trip over. Queen Victoria would not have approved I'm sure.

The other great event for Mullion in 1952 was the arrival of the heart throb film stars Clark Gable and Gene Tierney and a film crew. They were there to make the film 'Never Let me Go'. A love story set in the cold war between the West and Russia, quite a controversial film of its day. The film crew took over the cove for several weeks. Everyone turned out to watch the filming and my mother said she watched take after take of Gable having to run up the steps at the side of the harbour wall until he was exhausted. Possibly a pay back from the director for the hours and hours wasted each morning waiting for the Stars to appear from the hotel where they happened to be staying together .

My parents used to make ships in a bottle on winter evenings and one was borrowed by the director to use as a ship on the horizon. I still have it with a very faded Clark Gable autograph on the bottom of the bottle.

The film came out in 1953 but I'm not sure how long it was before it came to Cornwall. It must have been very exciting when it did.

As June approached in 1953, work started on the carnival float for us. It was a large flat farm trailer and was fitted with a purple and gold canopy held up on the four corners by sturdy posts plus one more post fitted behind a large ornate throne which would be where the newly to be crowned Elizabeth would sit.

At last Coronation day arrived, there were only a handful of black and white televisions in the village so people were either packed into sitting rooms to watch a blurry version of the great procession on a tiny screen set in a big cabinet, or for the rest of us, we listened to all the pomp and circumstance on the 'steam' radio. We listened in awe and silence and there was much cheering when Elizabeth was pronounced Queen of England and the

Commonwealth.

There was bunting all over the village and in the cricket field trestle tables were set up for all the children who lived around and about. There was Kiaora orange squash, sandwiches and lots of cakes and then each of us was presented with a little model of the coronation coach and horses and a tin of smarties with a picture of the new queen with her husband Prince Phillip on the front. We were also each given a special coronation china mug. We had a wonderful afternoon.

The Womens Institute in the centre of the village doubled up each Saturday as our local cinema and as a special treat the Walt Disney film Bambi was to be shown for us children in the evening. We all trooped along and paid our sixpences plus a penny for a cushion and settled down to watch. Unfortunately there had been some mix up and the film we actually saw was Dicken's A Christmas Carol with Basil Rathbone as a very scary Scrooge. In fact I had night mares about it for many weeks afterwards.

The Saturday following the Coronation was Carnival day and at last we were able to get into our costumes and climb onto the ready trailer. Susan onto her throne, Queen Mary II standing behind her holding onto a post while the rest of us held on to the four posts at the corners which I can remember feeling incredibly excited about. I'm told that having been lifted up there and told to hold on very tightly and not let go, I said "Look at my dear little hand holding on" which for some reason became a bit of a saying for some years afterwards.

Our float was pulled by tractor from the farmyard where we had got on to it and we joined the procession which set off all around the village and back to the cricket field for judging. The carnival that year was amazing, every float had been worked on for months, there was even a full sized model of an elephant. The Six Queens of England triumphed and won first prize but also attracted a lot of attention from the press who were very impressed by so much work and attention to detail being done and felt that more should be made of our float than just one procession around Mullion village. And so it was decided that we would do a tour over the several Saturdays following of such towns as Redruth and Camborne, Helston and Porthleven, I'm not sure that we didn't even get taken to Penzance and Falmouth. We all loved the attention and excitement and many people came to watch as our regal procession passed by.

The summer of 1953 was moving well.

The school was growing and thriving again and the visitors bookings came in thick and fast. My mother who I am sure should still have been convalescing over those summer months, coped with all of her duties in the house, aided by my father and Uncle Ron. She still found time to take us girls to the beach for picnics and gradually we taught ourselves to swim in the safe environment of the harbour. My absolute love and passion for the sea was born then and has remained, I can remember the agony of being told that the sea wasn't warm enough to swim from early April when the days were bright and the sea seemed so tempting . We had to wait until perhaps mid May when we dipped the first toe into freezing water. Now of course even in mid winter the surfers are out there, small black Lowrie-like figures kneeling patiently on their boards waiting for the next big wave. The surfers have become so skilful and the boards so stream lined, that they can surf on the smallest of waves as well as the huge breakers.

We would learn to swim in the harbour with a blown up rubber ring or simply float our bodies in the shallows where we could touch the sand underneath with our hands and pull ourselves along until we dared to lift them, or went slightly too deep and found ourselves floating unaided, not without a lot of water being taken in through the ears nose and mouth. There were no swimming lessons and no public swimming pools other than the tide filled man made pool at Penzance a long way off, so we all developed our own styles of swimming. I still get funny looks when I'm in a public pool as I practice my rather odd looking crawl or breast stroke but they get me along.

A whole new world would open up to us once we learned to swim. Seeing how many times we could swim back and forth from the harbour arm to the beach when the tide was in, jumping off the harbour steps and later off the top of the wall and then the joy of learning to body surf on swift wooden boards at Polurrian where there was often a good surfing day, the boards were very fast and manoeuvrable taking you right up onto the beach. We painted our boards with gloss paint, stripes and patterns and names of pop groups. I had Elvis and Cliff written on mine. To this day I feel a sense of slight suffocation if I am too far away from the sea especially on a hot day. I am never happier than when I am on in or next to water.

We would climb down the steep cliff path, loaded down with picnic and towels, costumes and bathing hats and perhaps a few bits of odd shaped wood roughly painted from our paint boxes, to represent boats. My mother would settle herself on the sand at the bottom of the slipway while we played in the stream and the edge of the water. We were quite excited if the picnic consisted of Cornish pasties as we didn't get to eat them very often but just smell the delicious aroma of them as they cooked in the oven.

One day we got down to the harbour as usual and settled ourselves down when a young man started to make his way down the slipway, walking on the uneven surface with considerable difficulty on crutches. He settled himself on the far side of the beach and proceeded to get himself ready for a swim. Once attired in his swimming trunks he began to unscrew one of his legs which he placed next to his towel. We children were utterly shocked and fascinated and my mother had great difficulty in getting us to stop staring wide mouthed at the man as he made his way on crutches and his one good leg towards the water. Once in the sea he swam strongly right out of the harbour and was gone for some time before returning and making his way back to his belongings. Soon afterwards we gathered up our towels and picnic, wet sandy feet planted

in our sandals and made our way slowly
back up the cliff path. When we got home
still feeling quite shaken by seeing the
man with one leg, our parents sat us down
and explained that the young man had
been very brave and fought for his country
in the war and had a terrible wounding
which left him with only one leg and so
they had had to make a false one for him
so he could walk again. I felt a little
comforted by the fact that the leg he had
unscrewed was not his real leg. As for the
war which had ended so comparatively
recently, to me at the age of five, it
seemed like something that had happened
in the dark ages.

Once we had achieved the glorious art of
being able to swim and float properly with
no aids, our mother would take us to the
cove and through the natural cave which
took you to the beach on the other side of
the harbour. You could only go through
the cave at low tide because at high tide
when the harbour was full, the cave also
filled with water. It was dark in the cave
and water dripped from the rocks above.
It was full of rocks and you had to be
careful as you picked a route through. As
you got to the centre there was a deep
pool, the most difficult part to negotiate
but once through, there was the wonderful
yellow beach where we would spend

happy days, playing in the sand and climbing about on the huge falls of shiny serpentine rocks. The rock pools were lined with pink crustaceans and we learned about all the creatures that dwelt within, limpets, winkles, big red sea anemones that looked like shiny German helmets, cockles and tiny shrimps and many types of seaweed. The sea outside the harbour had small waves and Wendy and her friends began to teach themselves how to surf on them, using their bodies as surf boards while we smaller ones played and basked in the deep warm sandy pools that formed around the big rocks. Our mother kept a close watch on the tide as it began to come up the beach and we usually went back through the cave just as the water was beginning to lap into the entrance. Most years there were accidents in the cave where people tripped and fell and we would hear the sound of the alarm bell as the big black St John's ambulance raced down to the Cove. Mercifully my mother managed without mishap, how brave she was to even attempt it so relatively soon after polio and a broken leg.

On Saturday mornings my mother, Wendy and I went into the village to buy a few extra groceries and some Saturday sweeties to eat, my favourites being Lucky

Numbers, while listening to In Town
Tonight followed by the Vic Oliver show on
the radio. The village stores were owned
by Mr Lugg, a very jolly man who every
Saturday would say to my Mother.
"Morning Mrs. Killick I see you have
brought your little boys with you today". I
think Wendy must have been old enough
to know it was a joke as she didn't seem
ruffled but every time I would get furious
"I'm NOT a little boy, I'm a little girl" I
would pout which of course made Mr. Lugg
tease all the more. Mr Lugg's daughter
was Sheila Tracy who presented Big Band
Special on the Light programme, now
Radio 2. She also played trombone in a
vocal/trombone duo known as the Tracy
sisters and was the first woman to read
the news on radio 4.
On the way home we stopped off at
Mrs.Nicholls corner sweetie shop to buy
spangles and sherbert dabs with our
pocket money and the packet of sweets
my Mother would choose for the evening.
Most of the food and house supplies were
delivered. There was the bread van, the
papers, the milk lady, the fish van, the
coal lorry, the butcher's van and the
laundry van. My mother ordered the
groceries by telephone, the order being
meticulously taken down by hand.
One afternoon a week Bert would arrive in

his big lorry. The lorry had been ingeniously converted from a dust cart with the big rounded sliding metal doors which pushed up originally for collecting rubbish, now revealing fruit and vegetables. Bert would always park just up the lane and come into the kitchen where my mother would give him her order and make him a cup of tea. He parked in a most convenient place as far as Wendy and I were concerned because we could go and climb up onto the high Cornish hedge at the side of the lane and pick fruit from the side of the lorry. Red cherries were our favourite and we stuffed ourselves full. We never got found out because we could easily hear when Bert was on his way back to fulfil the order as he began whistling as he left the kitchen. Our postman at the time was Harry, middle aged, cheerful small and wiry. His rounds must have been arduous. No formal streets to walk with short drives, Harry's rounds were on the cliffs and moors, following long tracks down to farms, climbing up and down steps in the cove and tramping paths that were unapproachable by van. He was fond of a tipple or two and entertaining the Grockles with his tall stories. One year just before Christmas when Harry's postbag was particularly weighed down with Christmas cards, he popped into the Old Inn in the midst of his deliveries and downed a few too many pints of Devonish. That afternoon my father happened to be walking down the lane beside our house when he heard a bit of a commotion. As he turned onto the road, there was Harry pulling handfuls of letters from his bag, tearing them up and throwing them into the wind. My father shouted to him to stop. He turned to my father and said "It don't matter what you do as long as you tear 'em up" and continued chucking the letters into the wind until my father was able to restrain him.

Somehow Harry's "Don't matter what you do as long as you tear 'em up" chant became a bit of a mantra locally and actually found its way onto radio where it became a catch phrase for Jon Pertwee in a comedy show called Waterlogged Spa where he played an old postman.

One particularly out of the way destination for Harry's van was a house built in a sheltered valley which looked out onto a different aspect of Mullion island where it now resembled the shape of a lion lying down and in fact around Predannack many people knew the island as Lion island. Pradnack Morva had a fascinating history. It was built almost single handedly by a naval Commander with five children, who in the nineteen twenties decided with his wife to leave London and bring the children up in clean air in the country. After much searching he found what he thought to be the perfect place set in a valley out on the cliffs between Mullion Cove and Kynance and having obtained enough land he began the arduous task of building a house big enough for his family. Before he could start building the actual house, a track would have to be laid leading out onto the cliffs from Predannack. The rough stony track survives much as it ever was and must be around a quarter of a mile long. Before starting on the main house Commander Halliwell first built a long wooden single story chalet, roofed with pig iron, where the family would live whilst he built the house. The house was thoughtfully architected with fabulous aspects from the seaward side. Inside Commander Halliwell built in some very clever labour saving devices. The delightful lounge was parquet floored and surrounding the fireplace the walls were of wood with built in recessed book shelves. The actual fireplace surround and hearth were of red brick and to the left was a small square wooden pull out door and behind that a supply of coal. In the wall just a little way up the stairs in the hall was a much larger square door. When the coal supplies were delivered, they were brought into the house and placed into the large shute behind the stairs door. The coal fell towards the small door by the fireplace thereby keeping a continuous supply by the fire, without the usual fetching and carrying from a coal store outside.

The upper part of the house on the seaward side overshot the ground area and was supported by pillars to the ground thus providing a sheltered area for sitting out and protecting the lounge to some extent from the mighty force of a Cornish gale.

Although Pradnack Morva was a house of singular design, it still retains an art deco look and over the years has been sympathetically extended.

Due to the steepness of the garden, the stony rutted drive meandered its way back and forth down to the gravelled area by the house. There were lawn areas built up around trench like grassy paths which was a novel idea but very impractical for mowing as the mower would have to be lifted onto the several small lawns.

It must have been with relief and delight that the family moved into the house at last after living in the overcrowded thin walled chalet which still survives at the top of the garden but life has a habit of kicking you in the face sometimes and so it was a cruel irony that having moved their family to the other end of the country to promote good health, their children contracted TB from the fresh jugs of unpasteurised milk obtained from local farms. Milk was a potent source of the infection for many people, particularly children for whom there was a high mortality rate. Eventually a law would be passed making it illegal to sell tuberculous milk and a tuberculin test was developed which could identify any infected cattle before they showed any symptoms. Herds began to be tested in 1935 but it was not until 1950 that eradication finally got going and it was a great success.

By the time my parents came to know the eldest daughter Jo who had inherited the house on her return from India with her husband Graham and two boys, tragedy had struck and two of Jo's siblings had died from the disease. Jo and her eldest brother Kit had also contracted TB but mercifully survived, her other brother John went down with his ship in the war.

Jo and my mother were to become close friends. My memories of Jo when I was a child were of her turning into the drive at Henscath in her cream coloured two seater sports car, she was thin and tall and had a wildly wicked look in her dark brown eyes, her voice very cultured and 'Darling'. Jo wore unusual alternative clothes, baggy trousers and a windcheater and cream silk shirts. She held a black silver rimmed cigarette holder. Goodness knows how strong her lungs must have been having managed to combat TB and now continuing to smoke heavily.

In fact Henscath kitchen was a slave to smoke. Either the boiler was belching out all over it or there was a constant blue haze from Senior service cigarettes and my father's pipe. I used to watch fascinated as the smoke tipped out over the top of the window which was only inches open.

The journey by foot from Henscath in order to reach Pradnack Morva was fairly arduous, the Cowley by now had chugged its last breath, or to be more precise had met with an untimely end over the side of a cliff and insurance money was paid out. I never knew the full story being that I was a small child at the time but I got the idea over the years from snippets of conversations in the kitchen, that although it was deemed to have been an accident due to the hand brake cable snapping, it was perhaps helped on its way a little. The truth of that we will now never know but from now on the family would be car less and journeys would have to be made by foot and the occasional bus service. The shortest route to the Morva was via cliffs and moors. Down the cliff path to the harbour and then up onto the moors, a very steep climb to the top followed by undulating cliff and moorland and hoping the wild horses were not in evidence on that part of the cliff as they were very unpredictable and prone to gallop at unsuspecting walkers. Eventually the chimneys of Pradnack Morva came into view and there would be a welcome cup of tea waiting for us.

More often it was Jo who came to Henscath and sat at the kitchen table, chain smoking and chatting to my mother as she prepared meals.

Jo's husband Graham had played a very large part in the electrification of India. He was a proud Scot and one of the most knowledgeable men I have ever known. They were an eccentric pair and while Jo ran about in her two seater sports car, Graham drove a large Rolls Royce with the memorable number plate of HUN 21. He didn't leave the house very much, he spent many an hour sitting by the fire reading heavy tomes on diverse subjects or adding to his impressive collection of homemade wine. There was barely a plant in the garden that wasn't put into a fermenting jar. Graham's homemade wine cellar was quite impressive, I remember one of the wines was called jungle juice and one he made with potatoes which apparently tasted of whisky with pretty much the same alcohol content. Graham had a gentle cultured Scottish accent and wore his kilt at any opportunity, he had a look of Alec Guinness about him and a very wry sense of humour which he shared with my father. He used the Rolls Royce mostly to take the dustbins up to the top of the garden on dustbin day and I used to join him to wash the car down in the ford at the bottom of Ghost Hill on the way to the village. Eventually I believe the car was bought by an American and shipped to America where perhaps it still exists, I really hope so.

Jo and Graham's two boys, Timothy and Donald were older than Wendy and me. They both went away to school and Timothy rarely returned to Cornwall after his schooling. Donald eventually did and became a close friend of our family. He was a large man with jet black hair and huge beard and a laugh like a giant. He became a sea Captain in the merchant navy but always came to spend time with us on his return from months at sea. He continued the tradition of slightly unsuitable cars and drove around in a little Isetta bubble car which he could only just fit into.

One of Jo and Graham's quirky ways was their deterrent for persuading moorland cattle away from the top of their garden. They worked out that by the time an air rifle pellet had travelled from their front door to the top of the garden it would not be going fast enough to penetrate a cow hide, just to sting it, so they would stand pinging air rifle pellets at unsuspecting cattle haunches which had the desired effect of making them turn and run. It was a thrilling day when my friend Kip and I were allowed to take our own pot shots at the cows backsides. I somehow doubt they would have got away with such practice these days.

Me with my father on the big day
(QV would definitely not have 'Been Amused')
Wendy following

Five of the Six Queens on the trailer

The Six Queens

L/R Marianne and Jane Dickinson,
Wendy, Susan Truscott, Maria Silk and Penny

CHAPTER EIGHT

Daffodils and Mullion Cove
1953

My father and Ron tried their hand at growing daffodils in the early fifties and had some small success while continuing to grow the field of anemones of ultramarine blue, mauve, purple, pink ,whites and reds. Backbreaking work to prepare the field, do the planting and then reap the flowers if you were lucky enough to get a good crop.

Although the generally milder Cornish climate is the perfect place for growing early daffodils, so much depends upon the weather when you are growing delicate flowers on a long narrow peninsula stuck out into the Atlantic ocean.

In Spring, coming upon fields of yellow, the colour of the dawn sun against a sparkling gold-flecked blue sea, is a truly breath taking and unforgettable experience.

The growing of daffodils is a highly competitive industry and come the picking season from January to May, many people young and old come to harvest the flowers which are sent on up country to Covent garden and beyond. The cutting is very specific and usually there are ten flowers to a bunch with an elastic band placed around the stalks. The experienced daffodil picker can earn good money over the season.

Such a critical time for the flower farmer. A field of daffodils or anemones hit by a sudden unusual frost or wintry gale can turn a field of golden yellow or the rainbow colours of anemones into a sagging brown mess within a very short time. The daffodil farmers get some sort of compensation but there are a lot of people who depend on daffodil picking to boost their income and they inevitably lose out.

Wendy and I loved the anemone picking time and went eagerly to help with the harvest. They were special days when friends and neighbours came to help pick in my father's small field on the edge of the village with no expectation of payment, their only reward being the vast picnic my mother would prepare. It was hungry work and once a good amount of flowers had been collected, we all sat with our backs to the high Cornish hedge out of the wind devouring pasties pies and sandwiches washed down with mugs of hot tea and bottles of Kia-ora orange squash. I couldn't honestly say that my sister and I were a great help, probably only picking three or four bunches between us until something else caught our attention but we felt part of it.

After several bad years of the crops being hit hard by unusually frosty winters when all the work to prepare and plant went to nothing, my father made the decision to give up growing flowers. It was all taking too much time away from his teaching and other duties anyway and unlike today when the flowers are sold at a premium, there was not much margin for a decent profit in the fifties. The field was too small to be used for much else and soon filled with brambles, primroses and the odd surviving daffodil and anemone plant.

We went there the following year, this time to pick blackberries.

Mullion Cove being an area of outstanding natural beauty, attracts many holiday makers each year and has also been used many times in films and television programmes the most recent in 2015 being 'And then there were none,' the Agatha Christie thriller where amongst the many stars were Charles Dance, Aiden Turner and Miranda Richardson. Mullion Island was the focal point for the production and I watched some of the filming from up on the cliffs. The sea was quite rough and the actors had to get into an open boat which was pulling a small tender full of suitcases to be filmed heading for the island. I wouldn't have cared to be in that boat and when they returned, the suitcases in the tender were awash. All very exciting and I imagined the local people standing probably in the same spot as me sixty three years before watching Clark Gable and Gene Tierney acting their way onto the big monochrome screen.

Mullion Island sits some half a mile away from the harbour, uninhabited other than by the thousands of sea birds who rear their young on it each year. The soil is manured by the sea bird droppings and sea beet and mallow flourish, in early summer the island takes on a purple hue when the mallow is in flower. I only ever went there on one occasion when our neighbours, the Ladners, invited Wendy and me to go with them on their small clinker built boat one calm sunny day in Spring. Once safely on to the rocks at the bottom of the island they soon realised their mistake in coming at that time of year. The Island was littered with gull, guillemot and cormorant fledglings, you could hardly put a pin between the nests and it was difficult not to tread on them. We were soon being dive bombed by angry parents. We had to grab old dead stalks of mallow plants to wave above our heads while we made a hasty retreat back to the boat.

In the days of pilchard fishing, a huer (lookout) would be placed on Mullion Island to watch for shoals of pilchards and alert the fishermen. The Cove has its once thriving pilchard industry to thank for its sheltering harbour walls. The harbour was completed in 1895 and financed by Lord Robartes of Lanhydrock who owned Predannack Wollas Manor from the 1600s . The harbour was built as recompense to the fishermen following several disastrous fishing seasons.

Like the Welsh, Cornish people love to sing and the harbour has long been used for hymn services on its sturdy walls. It is incredibly stirring to hear forty or fifty Cornish men singing lustily in the clear air while the sea laps against the walls.

The Cove has always been loved appreciated and used. The pilchard industry declined but there have always been crabbers. Auntie Nellie's husband Glen and his brother Jack owned a crab boat going out in all weathers. In the winter when it became impossible to take their boats out, the crab and lobster fishermen would congregate in the old pilchard net store, now a listed building, to mend nets and make and repair crab and lobster pots and no doubt recount tales of the sea. In the fifties and sixties the leisure sports were rock climbing diving and swimming. Each August during Mullion Carnival week there was water sports day. Everyone thronged to the cove to watch from the cliffs and fill the harbour walls. There were two cafes, the Porthmellin and the Gull Rock which on water sports day were bursting at the seams with business. The delightful Porthmellin cafe survives but the Gull Rock has long since been converted to a private dwelling. There were swimming races for all ages and various games, a greasy pole was constructed out from the harbour wall near the lighthouse, the grease being treacle black. Two daring contestants would edge their way along it clutching pillows and proceed to bash at each other until one fell off into the water. Goodness knows what the grease might have been, it was incredibly slippery and the daring contestants remained covered in black for the rest of the day despite their inevitable dunking in the sea.

I swam in the races as I got older but never dared to get onto that high greasy pole. There was great excitement when the Lizard lifeboat hove into view and sailed into the harbour. But the biggest highlight of the day was the boat race around the island, in which boats of every description took part. The magnificent powerful motor launch Pinda always won even though she was given a greater handicap each year.

Over the years and now that water sports have become more and more popular, there is snorkelling, coasteering, kayaking and paddle boarding. Gig racing has become more and more popular over the years and particularly with schools participating. The pilot gig is a thirty two foot long six oared rowing boat, built originally as a general working boat. There is evidence that these boats were used for rescues as far back as the seventeenth century. The boats have always raced although previously in a much more serious way when several pilot boats would strike out to reach incoming vessels and whichever one got their pilot on board first would get the job and the payment. The Isles of Scilly hold gig races on the first May bank holiday weekend, one of the busiest times on the Scilly calendar. The new Mullion Comprehensive school currently dominates this sport in the area.

From a very early age all the local children were taught to respect the force of the sea and the danger of the cliffs. It is a respect that never leaves you and sadly reinforced by the not uncommon fatalities from people swimming out too far and getting caught in rip tides or getting too close to the edge of crumbling cliffs and falling from them. There were some fatalities too from rock climbing. Of course as kids with the huge amount of freedom we had, we did do dare devil things which make me wince now at the thought of how dangerous they were but we knew what our bounds were and in the main we didn't abuse them. I was nowhere near as adventurous as Wendy who could walk along the narrow ledge half way down the seaward side of the harbour wall and once climbed to the bottom of the cliff from the car park outside the hotel. It was far more hazardous and scary than she had imagined and she was lucky to make it up to the top again without me having to go for help.

Our kids playground were the moors and cliffs, the harbour and through the cave. Several of our friends and school chums lived in the caravan field down the hill from Henscath opposite the quarry. With the interruption to careers and the inevitable difficult financial situations some people found themselves in since the war years, living quite cheaply in a caravan gave them the chance to pull themselves up again and save to put a deposit on a house. The caravan field was a part of Hannibal Williams small farm. It was sheltered and the mill stream ran along one side. Once it had been used to turn the big mill wheel at the farm as it headed for the sea, there we caught tiddlers and tadpoles in the Spring. On reflection Hannibal was kind and patient with us kids, he lived with his mother in a cottage behind the mill stream on the Cove road, I hope we were nicer to him than I remember and maybe thanked him sometimes for letting us ride on the big red wooden trailer towed by his black carthorse Captain, after he had collected the silver metal dustbins from the caravans to take to the rubbish dump at the top of the steep rough cart track. No health and safety then, we just sat amongst the rattling bins or swung our legs over the side. It was just heaven. Occasionally Hannibal would let us ride on Captain's broad back as the magnificent beast bent to the task of pulling his heavy load.

Sometimes we would get up really early to go and help round up the cows from the fields above the farm and steer them down the tracks to the milking parlour where Hannibal and his mother milked them all by hand. Every cow had a name and its own milking stall, as they entered the milking parlour each would find her own place. We took the task very seriously and I think were an actual help because as we grew older, we were sometimes allowed to collect the cows by ourselves and return them to the fields after milking.

On one occasion Hannibal decided to put a few of his herd in the middle of the caravan field with a square of electric fencing around them so they wouldn't wander up to the caravans. He said he wanted to keep an eye on them as one of the cows was about to produce a calf. We were all very excited at this prospect, not quite knowing what to expect and we stayed around all day hoping to see the calf being born. Sure enough in the late afternoon there was a bit of a commotion amongst the small herd as one very fat cow lay down and Hannibal arrived to make sure all was well with the birthing. After a while a grey slippery looking package slipped onto the grass at the back of the cow who turned and licked at her baby until the after birth was removed and the tiny animal got slowly to its wobbly feet. The cow then proceeded to eat the after birth by which time the calf had found his mother's teats and was having his first feed in the open air. We kids watched in fascinated silence knowing absolutely nothing about such things. It all seemed so natural and rather beautiful.

We played in the old flour mill which had three floors with rickety stairs. There were sacks of flour and barley and I'm sorry to say that we played with their contents, throwing handfuls over each other as we climbed the stairs. On one occasion I was hiding near the top of the stairs with a big bucket of cereal. I heard footsteps and I threw the lot as hard as I could. The footsteps belonged to Hannibal whose head appeared above the stairs. He looked like a ghost, covered as he was from head to foot in the white flour. Of course I thought I was in for big punishment but he just told us quietly to leave the sacks alone and took his leave. We were very lucky he didn't tell our parents and we never touched the sacks again.

Hannibal was happy for us to play hide and seek in the hay barn where we tried to chase the frightened rats and mice and made tunnels in the hay. I don't remember any of us suffering from hay fever.

We remained pretty much unscathed other than the inevitable bashed knees and bruises . It never occurred to us to be scared of anything apart from one particular very scary occasion.

One summer evening our dancing teacher

Nickie who lived in a mobile home in the caravan field next to the mill stream, invited all of us children and parents to a barbecue. Afterwards while the grown-ups chatted and drank and as dusk approached, we kids took off for a few games in the hay barn. We opened the big grey slatted door as we always did, careful to close it behind us as we had been told to do, and flung ourselves into the hay, climbing the bales to get to the top. As I moved my hand across trying to get a hold of some baling twine, I felt something hard under my hand which I did not recognise as anything I would expect to find there. I moved the hay out of the way and realised it was a man's shoe but not only that it was attached to a man who was asleep in the hay. He didn't stay asleep for long as we all screamed, rushed for the door and fled back up the caravan field. We all jabbered at once to tell our various parents until someone said. "Ok kids off you go and play, come back when we call you" It was obvious that they didn't believe us but we persisted and eventually my father was persuaded to come with us to see. By the time we got there of course the man had gone but in his hurry had left a few bits of food and empty bottles and it was quite obvious someone had been there.

Poor chap it turned out he was just a gentleman of the road looking for a comfy night's sleep but it was a long time before we dared to go back into that hay barn. We wove complicated stories for games of knights in battle with metal dustbin lids for shields and sticks with points fashioned from penknives for javelins, or cowboys and Indians with wigwams made from old curtains and pinched bean sticks.

One time as we took a track up onto the moorland, bearing shields ready for battle, one of the more adventurous boys, Neil struck out into some thick gorse and heather as he thought he could see something worth investigating. What he found was a neat stone wall, not very high and curving as if it must have been a huge circle at one time. Inside the wall was the top of an elm tree amongst other brush, so whatever was on the other side had to be pretty deep. We climbed carefully over the wall and clinging to the branches of the elm, lowered ourselves down into what appeared to be the best den we could ever have hoped to find. It was like being on the inside of a huge ball. The ground was like a large bowl, it looked a bit like pictures we had seen of a Roman bath but this had been some sort of earth working. Around the edge was another stone wall above which the top was flattened earth

up to the inner walls. The earth centre
was slightly spongy and we scared
ourselves by thinking we might fall
through it. Over the top of this strange
place, the trees and scrub met to form the
top of the ball and making the whole place
quite dark. We decided to keep this den a
secret as instinct told us that possibly we
should not have been there but it was so
perfect for a secret meeting place that we
did not want to risk being told that we
could not go there. It was even quite dry
when it rained. It was most probably a
small copper mine or something at one
time but I don't really have much idea. I
have looked for it years later, I know
where it is but the amount of scrub
brambles, gorse and heather, make it
impossible to get to now.
Wendy and I loved to visit Jane and
Marianne in their caravan. After the
draughty corridors of Henscath, it was
delightful in the winter to sit in a cosy
caravan warmed by a paraffin heater or
calor gas stove and read comics or play
games of Snap and Happy Families. If we
needed the loo it was an Elsan, a free
standing portable toilet with a removable
bucket that contained chemicals which
was situated in an asbestos clad spidery
shed out at the back of the caravan. You
had to dare yourself to go there as you

took the risk of running into a ghost in the dark, ghosts were the one thing we kids were unanimously scared of and believed in wholeheartedly. It was good to get back to the warmth and security of the inside of the caravan after a visit to the loo. There were some spidery loos in a small breeze block building at the end of the field but no shower block. There were no bathrooms in the caravans either so it was a strip wash in an enamel bowl in the kitchen sink. It never occurred to me how much the parents especially must have longed to luxuriate in a nice hot bath. Occasionally in the summer they would place a zinc bath outside the caravan and surround it with boxes and deckchairs for modesty sake, then fill it with warm water and bath themselves in the garden. That must have been sheer luxury for them. We just thought it was great fun and very funny too.

Sometimes in the winter Wendy and I would go and play with the two sisters Sarah and another Wendy who lived in the imposing Mullion Cove hotel. There were few or no visitors in the winter months so we played hide and seek over several floors or filled baths to the brim with cold water and played with colourful toy submarines to which we added baking powder in order to make them go up and down in the water. The submarines came free inside boxes of cornflakes. I loved to wander around the kitchens looking at the big pans and ovens and king sized Maggie tins of soup or the containers of colourful jelly crystals and sugar which we would dip our hands into and eat like sweeties. Once the tins were empty we used them as stilts, my father making a hole in each side of the tin and fixing string to them. We stood on top of the tins and moved forward by pulling up on the string, slow progress but fun.

A small staff were kept in the hotel over winter to keep the place clean and a very loyal man called Dick ran the bar for the occasional locals who came in. Dick was a kind man and used to make weird bright pink cocktails for us with lots of cherries, non alcoholic of course but we loved them. However he couldn't resist having a bit of fun with us sometimes. A few years beforehand Dick had had an accident with a champagne cork which had come out with a force straight into his eye. He now wore a glass eye which occasionally he would take out and show us. I found it very scary and horrible but we had to be polite and pretend to laugh as he wished us to. He knew he was scaring us of course and he would appear upstairs where we played hide and seek and chase us with his glass eye in his hand.

As Spring approached, French fishing boats from Brittany would anchor outside the harbour seeking shelter. The Breton fishermen would row into the harbour bringing with them a French onion seller, bike and all. The old chap would cycle around the cove and the village with strings of onions tied to his bike and sell them to whoever would buy. The French fishermen patronised the Cove hotel where they would meet in the bar with our local fishermen where they would manage to converse and understand each other's dialect.

There were often huge tankers to be seen near the horizon, heading for America or the big natural harbour of Falmouth for repairs. A few times a year the beautiful three chimneyed ocean liner, the Queen Mary, as distinct from her sister liner the Queen Elizabeth which had only two chimneys, could be seen on the horizon heading for America.

Sadly sightings of large vessels were not always happy events and in 1967 the SS Torrey Canyon would sink off the Cornish coast spilling 120,000 tons of crude oil into sea with catastrophic consequences to sea life and the environment.

Sadly there has been many a loss of boat and life around the Cornish coast over the years but due to the amazing efficiency and braveness of the many life boat men and women stationed around the coast line, the toll is much lower than it could have been.

New Year's Eve was an extremely special time for us in Mullion Cove. Sarah and Wendy's parents who owned the Cove hotel, put on a very special evening for children and for the grown-ups. It was dinner suits and evening wear and the children had to dress in their best party frocks too. First of all in the early evening there was a black and white film for us children in the ballroom such as Calamity Jane where I thought the Deadwood Stage was going to burst right out of the screen on top of us. Then there was party food and games while the adults had dinner. After that everyone got together in the ballroom to dance the night away to the Blue Aces band and do the Conga all around the hotel. There was a lounge set aside for us young ones if we got tired and Dick would bring us pink fizzy drink with straws and thankfully on those evenings, kept his glass eye firmly in place. At midnight we waited to see a dark haired man carrying salt, coal and bread come through the door. Then there would be Old Father Time with his scythe as the clock struck twelve and one year my sister was asked to jump through a hoop covered in tissue paper to bring in the New Year. After that a big net of balloons were let down while the band played Auld Lang Syne. Then it was a piggy back ride on our parent's shoulders home to bed.

Betty and Q outside the Mullion Cove Hotel circa 1959

CHAPTER NINE

School, Guests, Dogs and Donald
1956-1958

Henscath school had been running now for several years and had gained a good reputation locally. My father had great success in getting children through the eleven plus and my mother had all her little ones reading fluently by the time they went up into my father's class at age five or six.

In September 1956 Wendy, having passed her eleven plus exam went on to the Grammar School in Helston, catching the bus from outside the hotel at the top of the road to make the ten mile journey each morning and returning on the afternoon bus. She seemed so grown up suddenly in her navy blue pinafore dress, white and navy striped blouse and maroon blue and gold tie. Over this she wore a navy blazer and navy beret. I was in awe but would have to wait another four years to join her.

As it turned out, Henscath school would be the only school that we attended together because by the time I was eleven Wendy, whose love of dance never faltered, won a scholarship to Elmhurst ballet school in Camberley Surrey where she progressed into a fine dancer.

The guest house was also running well and many of the guests came back to Henscath year on year becoming good friends with my parents. There were certainly some eccentrics as well. One year a young man booked a single room for himself. He was very particular about where he would like his towel placed. His early morning cup of tea had to be left outside his room at a certain time and he was extremely particular about the placing of his knife and fork and napkin etc. One of my little jobs in the summer was to go and turn the beds down for the guests whilst they had their evening meal. This involved folding down the bedspread and folding a corner of the sheet and blanket down enough for the guest to get into bed. This was done in the young man's room but the next morning he asked if the bottom of the bed could be folded right back each night as well as he didn't like his feet being covered up. He was pleasant enough and enjoyed his stay, commenting particularly on the high quality of the food which pleased my mother very much when she discovered at the end of his stay that he was butler to the Duke of Bedfordshire.

From the first year the guest house was open a Mr and Mrs Dorian came to stay at

Henscath every summer, all the way from Glasgow. Mr Dorian, balding, middle aged and quite stout, was a headmaster. His platinum white blond wife was a few years younger and very attractive, we thought she was quite bold for appearing at the dinner table wearing trews, Scottish tartan trousers, with her blue twin set and pearls. They always brought one of the teachers from Mr. Dorian's school, one Miss Tynan, a short rather nervous looking young spinster, who was a great friend of theirs. Mr Dorian and Miss Tynan did not drive and so Mrs Dorian drove the whole way in their old Hillman. The day of their first arrival, Mrs Dorian turned up the lane, discovered she could not negotiate the gateway to Henscath and got out of the car to come and find my father. She explained to him that although she could see that it would be necessary to reverse in, she had never actually been able to locate the reverse gear on the gear stick and had therefore never reversed the car. Each evening after dinner the Dorians and Miss Tynan would retire to the lounge to play scrabble until very late into the evening. One year there was a big argument over the game and Miss Tynan never returned with the Dorians to Henscath. There was no explanation made but clearly it was to do with that game of Scrabble.

A last minute booking for one night came in the form of the Minack Players, a small troupe of touring actors. My mother thought they all looked as if they could do with a good meal and stacked up their plates. The evening meal was eaten with relish by all of them with not a scrap left on their plates. The next morning they all asked for boiled eggs for breakfast, when they had finished they all asked for another egg. It wasn't until my father was clearing the tables after they had gone that he noticed there was only one egg shell in each place. It would seem that the troupe were finding it difficult to live on their small takings and had taken an extra egg each for later in the day.

A few families brought their dogs with them and sometimes I would be given the chance to look after them for a day when they went out to somewhere not suitable for dogs. I loved the responsibility I was given, taking them for walks over the cliffs with my friends and their own dogs. Bruno was no longer with us and Lucifer was not the most receptive of pets. Strangely, with my mother's very strong phobia about mice, Wendy and I were allowed to keep pet mice as long as they were not brought into the house. My father made some mouse cages and we kept the mice in one of the old pigsties which we now used as a play house and called it the Cabin. We had four mice in all, two black ones and two white ones and all was fine until we were asked to take on four more mice by a local family who were emigrating to Canada.

Within three weeks we discovered a batch of little pink plastic like babies with greeny coloured eyes which grew very quickly and soon another batch appeared. It was obvious that we would soon be overrun with pet mice and my father explained that the mice were going to have to be dealt with. He stood over the water butt where he drowned the brand new babies with tears streaming down his face, it was the only time we ever saw our father cry. Although of course he explained his tears away with excuses.

It was decided not to tell our mother about the sudden mouse population explosion and my father was not prepared to drown the twenty or so mice who were now growing their fur coats and had their eyes open. He made a couple more cages but still the new babies kept arriving.

One afternoon we had fed the mice and were picking up random ones to play with, when we were called for tea. We dashed off and on our return we found to our horror that in our haste we had left all the cages open and every mouse had escaped and disappeared. Now we imagined a small army of black and white mice heading straight for the kitchen and our mother running for her life but oddly we never saw a single one of them again. They probably made good prey for the buzzards or had the good sense to run in the opposite direction. It only occurs to me now for the first time in all those years to just wonder whether it was actually us who left the lids open and why we never saw so much as one pet mouse again.

There were several cats that roamed around the coastguard cottages, mangy looking and thin and I took to trying to look after them as well as I could, sometimes pinching a tin of Kittycat food from Lucifer's stock when they cried piteously for food.

Wendy and I also had imaginary horses which we took very seriously and became very real to us, feeding them and mucking out and riding them across the cliffs to Polurrian and back. But none of this was going to satisfy my hankering for a dog of my own.

Eventually I must have worn my parents down and finally it was agreed that we would take a dog from the RSPCA. I couldn't choose a dog as the RSPCA was a long drive from us and we were now car

less and so one afternoon a large RSPCA
van pulled into the drive, Max, ten months
old sat in the back of the van between a
bowl of biscuits and a puddle, his head
hung low.

"Last people we took 'im to, said 'e dint
suit 'em", the driver informed us as we
signed his chitty.

He drove away leaving the dog in our
hands. A medium dark coated short
haired dog with treacly eyes, he seemed
as pleased to see us as we to see him.
After a walk and lots of attention he
collapsed into his new bed by the boiler
and went to sleep.

My father came in to attend to the boiler.
As he reached across Max, the dog leapt
up snarling, baring his teeth into a
terrifying smile, sinking them into my
father's arm which luckily was covered in a
thick coat sleeve so the wound was
minimal.

We decided it must have been the shock
of seeing someone suddenly bending over
him that caused Max to behave this way,
as he then reverted to his good behaviour.
Then it was the turn of the milkman,
bending to put the bottles outside the
back door, this time Max drew blood and
the following day the postman was only
just able to ward him off with a stick
threatening to call the police.

After another incident with my father who bent to stroke him and narrowly missed having his face bitten, my Mother regretfully decided we would have to call it a day and have the dog taken away. The risk both to the family and the school children was too great. The RSPCA said they would send out an Inspector. He duly arrived and my Mother warned him not to touch the dog as he evidently did not like men.

"Oh he'll be ok with me" said the Inspector as he bent down to stroke Max who licked him and sat beside him as they drank tea while discussing the situation.

"You see he just needs to settle in" he said, stroking him.

My Mother looked doubtful.

At that moment a leaf from a pot plant next to Max, fluttered to the floor and the Inspector leaned over to pick it up; immediately Max turned into a raging snarling menace and flung himself at the Inspector, biting him in the leg. It was game over.

Max was last seen once again in the back of the RSPCA van but this time no biscuits and no puddle, just a very sad dog on its way to a sadder fate. It was a horrible decision to have to make and perhaps if my parents hadn't had the school children they may have tried to overcome this problem but they couldn't take any chances that he might bite a child in their care or indeed their own.

A few weeks later the RSPCA van rumbled into the drive again, this time containing a small ginger/yellow puppy which looked barely old enough to have left its mother. He had been with a large family who were evidently uninformed as to how to look after a puppy and the children apparently had used him more as a toy than a live animal. No cruelty intended but evidently he had suffered enough to be frightened of everything around him.

He was full of worms and fleas and malnourished when we took him over. He was to be my dog as I had pestered and pestered my parents for a puppy of my own.

Bengo was to grow into a medium sized dog. Short coat, soft pretty face and a twirly tail like a Basenji.

Once again we had got ourselves a very strong character who valued freedom at all costs as he grew into maturity and had that same mad glint in his eye that Bruno had and once again we had to resort to the lead on the clothes line to keep him at home. Unlike Bruno he accepted the restriction of the clothes line, he just waited patiently until he saw the next chance of escape.

I thought he was quite a clever dog but Jo always said he was "eleven-pence in the shilling" completely bonkers and on reflection she was probably right. He learned quickly but had his own ideas of how to carry out the rules. He could possibly have been a gun dog had he had the training, as his greatest love was to retrieve anything thrown for him and at any cost. A carelessly thrown rubber ring flew over the edge of the cliff one time and Bengo followed it without hesitation all the way down through the thrift grass and samphire which clung to the granite and on down to the jagged serpentine rocks below. We hardly dared catch our breath as we moved gingerly, ever respectful of the crumbling edges to peer over, only to see the nimble dog finding foot holds and zigzagging back up, tail wagging and with the precious chocolate smelling ring in his mouth.

He was not a fat dog but he was incredibly greedy, once he devoured all of the bowls of banana and custard for the school children's deserts which were waiting on a trolley in the kitchen and once a whole plate of homemade fudge which had been left to cool. Wendy said he deserved to be very sick after that lot. No sooner said than done, Bengo walked over to her and was promptly sick in her lap.

The shorter harbour arm sloped down to the harbour entrance at that time, very steep and high but this did not deter Bengo from following seagulls off the end of it and skidding down into the water, having to swim the length of the harbour to get back onto shore, or across to the steps of the longer arm.

Sitting on the slipway one hot day with belongings strewn around, the sea crept up and took one of my flip flops. My friends and I were dressed ready to go home and the flip flop was drawing out of the harbour with the tide. We ran up onto the long harbour arm with Bengo at our heels and pointed to the flip flop now floating out into open sea and told Bengo to fetch. It only took a few fervent commands for him to realise there was something in the water and in he went, paddled straight out and brought it back to the harbour steps. This then became a great game over the summer, throwing flip flops as far out of the harbour as we could and he never tired of it.

Bengo's greatest talent though was a real crowd puller. Being so fearless in the water, he thought nothing of coming out into the surf with me and was quite adept at leaping the waves. However one day I had gone out too far with my wooden body board and the waves were becoming menacingly big and finding their peak as they reached me so I had to strive out further diving in through the base of the wave in order not to become engulfed by it and I was beginning to feel a little frightened. To my horror I then realised that Bengo had accompanied me to that point. I yelled at him to go back but he just stayed around me. There was nothing I could do. At last a wave came that I felt could take me into shore without breaking over me. I was out of my depth which made things more difficult but managed to jump on and start frantically hand paddling with the wave. After a few moments I felt a searing pain on the backs of my heels although there was nothing for it but to carry on to shore, I remember crying and praying that somehow Bengo would find a way to get back. So it was with some surprise that as I got up from the shore foam, a small crowd had gathered and I turned to find Bengo shaking himself vigorously with that insane smile of his on his face. The backs of my ankles were very bloodied, the reason being that Bengo had unbelievably hitched a lift using the backs of my ankles as a hook to grab onto with his claws and somehow managed to hang on all the way.

When I recounted the tale to my parents,

my father took the surfboard and fixed a metal ridge on the end of it for Bengo to hook his claws on to. The surfing dog became quite a show stopper that summer. I didn't go so far out and made sure that he had positioned himself behind me before catching the wave. He never missed, we must have been a very comical sight.

He was not an aggressive dog in the normal way apart from the fact he was a bully with other dogs and was extremely protective of me and my friends and so if we left our belongings on the beach a little too close to another pile of picnic and belongings and he had chosen to stay on shore while we swam, he would bark and snarl at the owners of the towels next to ours as they returned up the beach to use them. This often ended up badly and we would get a good telling off as we came out of the water.

One summer's day Bengo arrived home with a beach cricket ball in his mouth which he deposited at my feet. Shortly afterwards a large sweating man walked by the kitchen window clad only in shorts and sandals. His upper body and bald head, pillar box red with sunburn, his large stomach spilling over the shorts. He banged on the open back door and Bengo jumped up and barked at him. The man snarled back "Your dog stole our cricket ball" . You should keep him under control". Evidently he had followed Bengo up the steep cliff, determined to get his possession back. I couldn't help but wonder if in his normal day to day life, he worked suited and booted in a prestigious bank somewhere in Surrey and what his colleagues would think if they could see him now, puffing and panting and reading me the riot act over a tuppenny halfpenny beach ball.

Of course I duly returned it to him and had a word in Bengo's ear and off he went.

Unfortunately that was the first of many such encounters but secretly I marvelled at the tenacity of the holiday maker following a dog half a mile up steep cliff paths to retrieve a replaceable ball.

Bengo would often return home from one of his forays limping badly. On inspection we would find his paws full of thorns. He must have had surprisingly tender pads for a dog. He would lie patiently on his back while we removed the thorns with tweezers, then lick us fervently in thanks.

As Bengo grew into old age, he would disappear for days at a time. The first time he did this we were frantic. Phoning the police and asking everyone to keep an eye out for him. We were convinced he had launched himself over one cliff too steep. But then to our amazement one morning, looking across the valley, there he was with a family in a caravan parked up on the moors, happily playing fetch a ball with one of the children. Apparently he had turned up unannounced one day and simply moved in with them. He came home again quite happily until the next time he got the wander lust and took himself off to another house or another camper for a few days.

As with all the dogs we had Bengo lived to a ripe old age and made our lives the richer for his sense of humour and grand bonkers character and the fact that we shared such a love of water.

For me, one of the most exciting days on the summer calendar was water sports day in the harbour and especially the boat race around Mullion Island. From the harbour, round the Island and back again was just over a mile. As a small child, I thrilled to watch those boats set out and desperately hoped that one day I could take part.

One year Donald arrived home on leave from the Merchant Navy, he was pleased to have progressed to the rank of Captain. He came to the house and told us that he had been planning to build his own boat to enter into the race. I was completely in awe of this idea and very keen to help. In typical Donald style he had decided to build the boat from his own imagination . He made a hastily drawn sketch with rough measurements but made no reference to text books. In his mind he had the picture of a second world war landing craft, rectangular, straight sided, with a steeply inverted sloping front. As far as I remember, the Hod was also flat bottomed, not really a sea worthy design altogether.

The Hod, as he named it was built in the garden at the Morva. I watched its progress eagerly and was happy to fetch and carry anything needed from the workshop. It was made entirely from heavy marine plywood, about twelve feet long with one bench seat across the middle and it was varnished to a dark mahogany brown. The front top was covered in ply to afford a store to keep belongings dry and to combat the forces of water. All in all it resembled as its name suggested, a large coal carrying hod. When it was finished and ready for its first launch, the trip to the Cove was in Pied Piper style. Slow progress, towed by a borrowed tractor and trailer down to the harbour, followed by practically every child in the village. The Hod was heavy and was rolled into the water over the logs used for pulling the fishing boats up the slipway, all of us kids pitched in to help. Donald waded into the water and climbed gingerly in. Being of heavy build, it seemed he might sink his precarious vessel but all was well, if sitting a little worryingly low in the water, as he edged to the central position. I passed him the heavy home made oars, one by one and he began his maiden voyage from one end of the harbour to the other and back. Progress was very slow and with no keel or prow, the Hod zig-zagged its way forward and eventually back again, mercifully without disaster.

It was nearing race day in carnival week and after a few modifications and the addition of a small outboard motor, the Hod lay ready and waiting on the slipway. The addition of the outboard made things even more precarious as the boat sat even lower in the water adding to Donald's bulky frame but amazingly it did stay afloat.

Race day dawned, a beautiful day with just the hint of a south westerly rippling the sea a little. Colourful bunting was strung all around and flapped gently in the breeze. The harbour walls and the cliffs teemed with people as the men prepared their boats for the start of the race. With so many different types of boat and power there had to be a handicap with the small craft starting way ahead of the larger. The first to go were any boats with a two stroke engine, small dinghies and suchlike, followed by four strokes and so on. The large open fishing boats with just an engine cabin were last but one, wonderful heavy clinker boats painted blue and green, as much a part of the harbour scene as the cliffs and harbour stones. Last to go was Pinda the crème de la crème of the one huge luxury powerful launch with a wake like a mini tidal wave which would have flipped any small boat within fifty yards at full throttle. Pinda's handicap that year was to wait until the first boats had actually rounded the island and appeared on the other side.

It was decided that the Hod should be the very first to leave. A loud speaker system was in place and Donald was given the go ahead with a klaxon which rang out across the water. The tide was high and the water was gently lapping up the slipway and so it was easy to push the boats in. With the little engine fixed securely onto the frame, Donald inched himself gently aboard and pulled his now remodelled lighter oars in with him. After several attempts the engine coughed into life, with much dangerous wobbling as Donald pulled the start cord. He was off with much clapping and cheering from the crowd. Fair to say we had plenty of time to watch his departure through the harbour mouth as progress was extremely slow. It was a comical sight, Donald's large frame, mass of black hair and huge black beard in such a tiny delicate vessel, a terror to any pirate ship, the complete antithesis to the ship he captained in the Merchant Navy. It all looked extremely vulnerable as he left the safety of calm water in the harbour and began bobbing up and down on the less forgiving open sea.

The next small dinghies and clinker boats lined up in the water, engines rattled and the klaxon again sounded for their start. There were around twenty of these small craft, mostly painted white and from the cliff top where I sat, they looked like balls of cotton wool floating in the green translucent water. There followed a bit of frantic jockeying for position as they entered the small gap between the harbour arms but they all made it through without mishap and within yards of leaving the safe haven of the harbour and entering more choppy water, they passed the Hod as it stoically zig-zagged its way towards the island.

By the time the largest colourful boats set out, all of the small boats were disappearing around the island, all that is save one, the Hod. The wind was beginning to blow harder and the Hod was bobbing up and down on the wavelets rather alarmingly, but still inching forward with her drunken snail like progress. Hard to see where she sat in the water now but at least she was still afloat.

The Island being so narrow and wide, it was a while before we saw the first craft appear round the other side but after several nail biting minutes the first few two-stroke boats appeared and now it was the turn of Pinda, gleaming white and with four or five passengers, how I wished I was one of them. Her engines thundered into life and she steered a beautiful arc as she left the harbour in pursuit of the last of the big fishing boats just disappearing around the back of the island.

It became difficult to see without the aid of binoculars as the sunlight glinted on the tips of the waves, or as the sun dipped behind a cloud and cast shadows and odd shapes over the white crests cradling the island's outcrops of fallen rocks.

Pinda was now well on her way, a huge bubble bath of white foam streaming out behind her. Even though she gave the still struggling Hod a very wide berth, it still rocked precariously in her wake for some minutes before battling on.

Several boats were now on the last leg back to the harbour and vying for position, the race well and truly on. The largest fishing boats comfortably passed many smaller craft, manoeuvering their way through them, the sea boiled white with so many wakes.

Several of the boats were well on their way back towards the harbour when Pinda hove into view from behind the Island. She had flown towards the island at an alarming speed skirting all in front of her with as much distance as she could and on the home straight she assumed the lead and came to a winning stop by the long arm steps followed by craft from every class as they clamoured for good positions for entering the harbour mouth. Great cheers went up, there was never a year when Pinda didn't win and each year she was given a greater handicap than the year before. She was expected to win and always did.

At last all boats were safely back in harbour. The tide was receding and with the harbour now only three quarters full of water, it was a tight squeeze. It was a wonderful sight and there was much laughter and cheering. At the end of the long arm, the Gweek silver band struck up with 'A Life on the Ocean Wave' and the podiums were put in place for the awarding of cups.

It was almost with one accord that everyone suddenly seemed to remember that there was one boat missing – the Hod – there was no sign of the Hod. Binoculars were cast across to the Island but the small craft with its large bearded occupant was nowhere to be seen. A message came over the loud speaker that a boat would be going out in search of the Hod. The obvious boat to go was Pinda although she was by now completely hemmed in by the other vessels around her and it took ten minutes to find a way safely through and out again to the open sea. There was silence in the Cove as everyone strained to scan the water but just as Pinda began to disappear around the left side of the Island, a great roar went up as the Hod was spotted rounding the rocks from behind the Island on the right and those with binoculars saw that Donald was rowing. Pinda drew carefully up beside the Hod , then after a few minutes, drew away from Donald and his coal scuttle, returning to the harbour. It seemed that Donald had run out of petrol with the over exertion of his small engine and was determined to get back by his own efforts. When, some thirty minutes later, he did join the other boats who cleared a path for him to the shore, the cheers were deafening and only yards from the shore, the listing, somewhat waterlogged Hod, gracefully sank in water only a few feet deep. I rushed down to join Donald as he waded out of the water and onto the slipway where he collapsed in a heap inviting the sun to warm him. "You should have worn a life jacket" I said, "everyone was very worried about you."

"I know" he said, "I really was beginning to wish I had ever learned to swim."

Donald Farquhar

Admiring the Hod at Pradnack Morva
L/R Penny Wendy, family friend Nibbie , Jo and Graham's
grandchildren, Donald's daughter Button, short dark hair,
Graham and my mother

Bengo

CHAPTER 10

More Significant changes
1958

One of the high lights of the year was Helston Flora Day, a magical Spring Festival which we always went to watch along with many thousands of people every year.

Because Wendy was now attending Helston Grammar School she was allowed the privilege along with all the other children attending Helston schools, of dancing in the Furry dance which falls on May 8th or the Saturday before if the 8th falls on a Sunday or Monday. There are several variations of the name and locally it is usually referred to as Flora Day. It is one of the most ancient of British customs and is still practised every year. It draws huge crowds, many people attending from all over the world.

Flora Day is a Spring festival to celebrate the ending of winter and the coming of spring, with all the new flowers and the greening up of the trees. The whole town is decked out with laurel leaves, yellow gorse and bright flowers such as bluebells and any wild flowers that can be found in season in window boxes and on lamp posts to herald the arrival of Spring. The dance is held whatever the weather and by the time it was my turn to join the procession the following year we all got completely drenched by rain but carried valiantly on to the end.

At seven in the morning a big bass drum beats and the first dance of the day commences. This is the first of three dances throughout the day that the adults will dance all through the town, in and out of shops and houses. The men in top hats and tails and the women in their finest frocks, a colourful sight. They all wear Helston's symbolic plant, the lily of the valley, the men wear the flowers on the left of their lapels and traditionally the women wear their posy of lily of the valley upside down on the right.

At eight thirty it is the turn of the Hal an Tow, no one knows the exact meaning of Hal an Tow but the nearest definition is 'Hoist the Roof' with men dressed in Lincoln green and Friar Tuck and Robin Hood are represented along with dancing flower girls. The main characters are St George and the dragon. In their procession around the town the players stop every so often to re-enact scenes of good against evil. The dragon gets to be slain by St George many times along the route. As they walk they sing an old traditional Cornish May Day song to

welcome the coming of summer but there
are also disparaging lines in the songs
against Spaniards which hark back to
1595 when the Spaniards raided Newlyn.
One of the verses goes:-
'What happened to the Spaniard
that made the boast so brave o.
That they would eat the feathered goose
and we would eat the roast o.
Chorus:-
Hal an tow
Jolly-rum-ba-low
We were up
long before the day o
To welcome in the summer
To welcome in the May o
For Summer is a coming in
And Winter's gone away o
We were all very excited to see Wendy in
her first Flora Dance.   The children's
dance began after the Hal an Tow at nine
forty. All the children wore white; for the
girls a white dress with colourful flowers in
their hair, a different flower for each
school, forget-me-nots, poppies or corn
flowers and the boys in white shirts
trousers and white shoes with only their
school tie to represent the school they
attended and lily of the valley for a button
hole.
Each year a different Helston school took
the lead in the children's processional

dance. The girls very much outnumbered any boys who might be persuaded to dance the streets with a girl whilst clad in white and wearing lily of the valley. But many boys did and most of the girls had to be content with dancing with each other.

Wendy had secured herself a handsome partner called John, there were well over a thousand children dancing in pairs, so it was hard to see her but there she was rounding the corner at the bottom of Wendron Street and I was thrilled. The dance is quite simple, more of a dancy sort of march and then a swing around with the next couple in front of you and back to your partner. There was a long way to go and some steep hills and in some of the houses it was quite difficult to negotiate your way in and out. In the fifties the music was provided by several silver bands at intervals between the line of dancers. The residents of Helston helped out by playing the music on gramophones from their upstairs windows. This made things a little difficult for the dancers as no band or record was actually playing the music at the same time but it didn't really matter as the spectacle of the children dancing through the streets all in their white is such an unforgettable experience.

The Flora dance continues and is as popular if not more so than it ever was. In the fifties there were approximately one thousand children dancing, now it is more like two thousand.

The Cornish have a fierce desire to keep traditions alive and the county is steeped in myth and legend. The Cornish language also lives and is taught in schools.

We collected Wendy after the dance from St Michaels gardens where they all finished and as a special treat we all went to the fun fair set up at the bottom of Coinage Hall street in the market place where there were swing boats, helter-skelters, a ghost train and dodgem cars. The day continued with the midday dance where the adults danced again in their finery and then they danced again at five pm after which everyone began to drift away. We didn't stay for the five-o-clock dance as it was a tiring day, the adults must have been pretty tired by their third dance in the early evening.

There would be two big events in 1958 which changed life at Henscath quite dramatically. The first concerned Uncle Ron who had now been living with us for over ten years.

The Blue Peter club in the village was owned by a very effervescent and likeable couple Johnny and Dorothy who had come to Mullion from somewhere in the Midlands. Johnny a diminutive man who enjoyed life to the full and welcomed club members with generous and open arms. Dorothy slightly taller than her husband with a fulsome figure and masses of blond hair managed the business side of the club whilst her husband played host and they worked very well as a team. My parents and Ron came to know them well through my father renting the small field from them for growing his anemones. Ron began to spend more and more time there and sometimes wasn't around for his guest house duties or arrived home only just in time full of apologies and slightly inebriated and argumentative.

It transpired after a few months that he had fallen deeply for Dorothy and was beginning to make himself a bit of a nuisance to say the least. Dorothy had no emotional interest in Ron and made it very clear but he persisted and in the end Johnny banned him from the club. Ron could not seem to walk away from this and started sending letters to Dorothy and calling her on the phone and of course word got around. Johnny made it very clear to Ron that he should leave Dorothy alone but he just could not seem to walk away from it.

One night as my parents were visiting the Old Inn, they heard that the Blue Peter club was on the market and Johnny and Dorothy were moving away back up country. Within a couple of months they had packed up and gone leaving Ron very depressed and he became more and more insular and bad tempered. Whether Johnny and Dorothy had left because of the nuisance Ron was making of himself or whether they just wanted a change of scene was never known but in the middle of the busy summer season Ron announced that he would be leaving Henscath and moving up country. Not only would he be leaving soon but he would be taking all of his furniture with him leaving my parents in a very difficult position as Ron's contribution to the furnishings and especially the beds, was being relied upon.

Wendy and I knew nothing of what was going on except that we sensed the fraught atmosphere and were aware that the grown-ups stopped talking if we entered the room.

Then came a very dark and scary day when a removals van turned up and collected all Ron's furniture including the beautiful black piano which I loved so much. We also loved Uncle Ron very much but suddenly it seemed he was going away and we didn't know why or where or if he would ever come back. All I remember of that day, was sitting in the lounge hall while grown ups rushed about and shouted. I don't remember Ron saying goodbye to us but I really hope he did. And then he was gone. I think Wendy had more of an inkling about what was going on as she was now coming up to fourteen but she was always very protective of me and probably decided to keep quiet about it.

I learned years later that when Dorothy and Johnny left to go and live in Leamington Spa, Ron decided he would go and live there too in case Dorothy were ever to change her mind about him, I never did know what happened but Ron was to come back and visit us several years later on his own and always sent Wendy and me a card with a pound inside it for Christmas and birthdays and the occasional postcard if he had gone away on holiday. It was a horrible time and as near to the feelings children must have when their parents split up as I will ever know. I felt betrayed and very sad and I expect I still do. The cards and money carried on arriving on our special days well into our teenage years until one year they stopped. We discovered sometime later that Ron had died alone in his Leamington

Spa flat probably as afraid to go to the doctors as he was the dentist.

The other significant event in 1958 was that Wendy would be leaving Helston Grammar School to go to Elmhurst Ballet School in Camberley. Our delightful ballet teacher Nickie Nicholson was well aware that Wendy's talents as a dancer needed more than she could give. She came to see my parents one evening and explained why she thought Wendy should be given the chance to mature into a professional ballerina. Nickie was impressed with the standards at Elmhurst and felt it would be the ideal school for Wendy. My parents could not possibly afford the heavy fees for such a prestigious school but it might be possible to win a scholarship there. And so it was arranged and borrowing Nickie's Standard 8 car we all trooped up to Surrey for Wendy to take the exam which hopefully would result in a decent bursary.

I had only been out of Cornwall once before when I was very small apart from the family's annual visit to Plymouth for new clothes and was fascinated by the leafy neat streets of suburban Surrey. We stayed with friends near Woking in a street where all the houses were almost identical, big houses surrounded by high fences and trees and the words 'Private

Drive No turning' next to the name of the house which tended to bear no resemblance to the building it described, such as Windermere or Hill Crest when there was no hill. I could feel a restricting atmosphere in the air but really it was just a completely different sort of place from the one I was so used to, it was kind of contained which Cornwall was not. Elmhurst ballet school was actually a number of different buildings set within beautiful gardens surrounded by rhododendron bushes and trees. Wendy was welcomed by Father John the head master and shown to the studio where she was to audition. I remember thinking she was very brave, it all seemed very austere to me and the teachers very lofty but after changing into the very specific leotard and tights required, she went in and performed her well practiced dance steps.

We returned to Mullion the next day and waited for the letter to come and after a few weeks, it appeared that Wendy had passed the audition with flying colours and would be due to begin her first term there in September. I had to be honest and admit to myself that a part of me wished she would not have passed but that was purely selfish and I kept it to myself. I couldn't bear to think we would be parted for three school terms a year.

Like many sisters we often fought like cat and dog but adored each other and the thought of her going away especially so soon after Uncle Ron's sudden departure, was hard to bear. It all seemed to have happened so suddenly and now here we were sewing Caches tapes into her sax blue uniform and onto everything she would be taking with her.

We had always shared a bedroom in order to free up as many rooms as possible for the school and the guest house and we were very opposite in many ways, she tidy and neat on her side of the room and in her clothes, me the opposite, always looking scruffy as was my side of the room but the bond between us could not have been greater and woe betide anyone who hurt either of us.

At last the time arrived in September for Wendy to go on her first long train journey to get to her new school. Graham arrived in HUN21 having freshly washed the wonderful old Rolls Royce in the ford, to take us all to Gwinear Road station to see her off. She had a large trunk which had been sent on ahead and just a small case with her initials on it to take on the train with her. My mother had made her a large picnic to eat on the train and the train guard agreed to keep an eye on her and make sure she caught the correct connection at Penzance which would take her on to Paddington where my parents great friends Nibbie and Doug who had become surrogate Aunt and Uncle to us children, would be waiting for her to take her to their London home in Chelsea for one night before transporting her to Camberley the next day.

I remember the journey back from Gwinear Road, my mother having managed to hold back the tears when we said goodbye, now let them flow freely and my father comforted her. Graham drove in his stately way, clipping the odd curb as he went and wisely keeping quiet while we all tried to collect ourselves. We waited anxiously for the phone call to say that Nibbie and Doug now had her safely in their hands and a tearful Wendy came on the phone but bravely said she was fine although she wasn't sure if she really wanted to go to ballet school after all.

It seemed to me an eternity until Wendy returned home for the Christmas holidays. Graham went to fetch her from Gwinear Road station, long since another casualty from the Beeching cuts. I went with him on that memorable trip in the musty car, me sitting in the back clinging to a twisted cord that hung from the roof and Graham who was not a tall man, peering up over the steering wheel giving a literal meaning to the phrase 'cutting corners' but we survived and I knew we were nearly there as we drove through the wonderfully named village of Praze-An-Beeble, excitement mounting as I set eyes on Wendy in her sax blue uniform and large straw hat which she had kept firmly on her head the whole way to Gwinea Road. Never had we been so pleased to see each other or had so much to talk about. Elmhurst ballet school still thrives, although it is now situated in Birmingham. There would be many goodbyes over the next ten years when Wendy went off to do summer seasons in this country or in Spain where she danced in Barcelona and Madrid. Sometimes returning home after a contract to spend six months or so with us working in an office which she could only tolerate for so long before moving on to another dancing venue.

Her first job was in a summer show in Paignton called 'Gay Time' without the connotations it would have today. The show was in a huge marquee on the front and starred Lester Ferguson the singer and Ann Emery sister of the comedian Dick Emery. Ann was equally as talented as her brother, a brilliant singer, comedienne and dancer but she never made it into the big time.

In 1958 the winds of change were

happening fast and life would be very
different during term times without my
dear sister there to keep me in check and
steer me in the right direction when I was
being wayward. I was ten and I knew that
one phase of my life had gone, now it was
time to knuckle down and try to pass the
eleven plus exam which would be in the
following January. Time to start to take
life a bit more seriously.
I would still attend ballet classes in the
Women's Institute in the village on a
Saturday morning and I loved tap dancing
but it was never going to be a consuming
interest for me.
We knew Nickie Nicholson from early
childhood. A vibrant dark haired attractive
lady who lived for ballet. She had been
married once and had two grown up girls
who had left home but now she lived in a
large green caravan next to the mill
stream in the caravan field with two young
girls she had become guardian to when
they became orphaned under particularly
tragic circumstances at a young age, their
father was a test pilot and was killed in a
plane crash, their mother who was very ill
at the time died soon afterwards in
hospital . Nickie took the two children on
without a second thought as was her
nature. The youngest child Lesley came to
Henscath as a pupil for a while, the eldest

Christine eventually went to the Lycee in Paris.

As a ballet teacher Nickie was very strict and achieved excellent results in the exams, Wendy achieving Honours in practically every exam she took. Nickie's strictness was only reserved for her classes however, she loved children and would frequently take a troupe of us up onto the moors for a makeshift barbecue or for a day on the beach with a big box of jam sandwiches and squash. Eventually she had a bungalow built on the other side of the village on the road to Poldhu but she lived in the caravan field for several years beforehand.

It was in 1958 that my father finally relented in his views about television. He had always thought televisions were a bad idea, an invasion on family life but with televisions in most people's houses by that time, he decided we should have one. It seems odd now that up to the age of ten I had barely seen any television at all.

One afternoon after school our longed for television arrived, a large wooden cabinet surrounding a small greeny grey screen.

It was so exciting and we were all glued to it that first evening. I remember watching Whirly Birds, the adventures of two Australian men in their helicopter, Champion the Wonder horse with Rebel the dog and the Lone Ranger in his mask with his faithful friend Tonto. It wasn't that easy to watch, it was black and white and we had terrible interference on the screen especially in the summer but it didn't really matter as long as you could get the gist of the programme. At least we didn't have the problem of choosing which channel to watch as there was only one which was BBC. ITV was not yet available so far South West. At seven o clock it was the Tonight programme with Cliff Michelmore, Derek Hart, roving reporters Fyfe Robertson, a tall Scot with a large beard and moustache and Alan Whicker just starting out on his long and illustrious career.

Fyfe Roberston came to Mullion Cove once and I managed to get his autograph, I remember how very tall he seemed and very kindly. Also on the programme was Cy Grant who used to sing sort of satirical calypsos on an acoustic guitar long before satire was popularised with David Frost on 'That Was the Week that Was'.

Our elderly neighbours next door, Connie and Bill Ladner held out against television for the rest of their lives and in fact did not even possess a radio. This was particularly odd because Bill Ladner had been one of Marconi's right hand men in building the apparatus for transmitting the first radio signals from Poldhu to St Johns Newfoundland at the turn of the century. There was a story that two officials turned up at Bill's house one day to check why he hadn't been paying for a radio licence and were ready to fine him. He told them he did not possess a radio but due to their knowledge of his work with Guglielmo Marconi they did not believe him and searched the house finding absolutely nothing.

The Ladners children had grown up and moved away, their daughter also a Penny, up country somewhere and their son a diplomat in the British consulate in Buenos Aires. Occasionally they came to see their parents but generally Bill and Connie lead a quiet fairly isolated life. The only times I remember going into their house was after they had been away for holidays when we were all invited in to see their holiday slides. We all settled into the lounge where Bill fiddled for ages with the projector and setting up the screen. I found it pretty boring as each slide had to be described fully before moving on to the next but I didn't mind too much as Wendy and I were always given a pot of broken pieces of Edinburgh rock to eat as we watched, a great treat.

Although the Ladners had taken Wendy and me on the abortive trip to Mullion

Island, they normally kept their little white clinker boat, the Gull, at Gillan and would sometimes take us for trips up the Helford estuary from there. I suppose if they were alive today they would be thought of as 'alternative'. Mr. Ladner would leave his car at the top of the rough lane and we walked with bags of swimming gear and picnics down to Gillan beach. Wendy and I would change into our bathing costumes modestly under towels but the couple would strip off completely in full view before putting on their costumes, Mrs Ladner in navy blue with frills and Mr Ladner in a lime green one piece as was the fashion then. We got used to their odd ways and they were very kind to us. Then we would help pull the heavy boat down to the water detaching it from its mooring buoy. The old couple climbed in while Wendy and I held the boat steady for Mr. Ladner to fix on the outboard motor and then we climbed in too and had a go at rowing until he had the engine fired up. Then off we would go through the clear green water hugging the jagged coast line into Gillan creek and back to St Anthony where Wendy and I would jump out for a swim, then out towards St Dennis Head and across the Helford river, quite choppy waters as we met the open sea heading for the little cove at the bottom of Trebah gardens where in 1944 the beach was used as an embarkation point for a regiment of several thousand Canadian troops for the assault landing on Omaha beach during the D Day landings. Here we would pull the boat up onto the beach and have a picnic on the warm slatey soft sand followed by another swim. Sometimes the Ladners would venture in with us but more often Wendy and I who were becoming strong swimmers would strike out to some moored yacht out in the middle of the river and back. They were wonderful days, quite rare and therefore the more precious.

I expect the Ladners missed their own children and enjoyed being able to take us out with them.

In the spring of 1959 my parents told us that a man would be coming to lodge with us at Henscath. I didn't know quite what to make of this, I didn't want someone to come along and take the place of my Uncle Ron which was how I saw it. My mother patiently explained to me that he wouldn't be taking Ron's place, only using one of the upstairs bedrooms as somewhere to live and would not be working in the house. He was a quantity surveyor and would be out most of the time. This I was able to accept and soon we were introduced to David Todd, a handsome young man who seemed very pleasant. He had a bit of an odd walk and my mother told me he had been involved in a terrible motorbike accident a few years before and we were to make no mention of his limp. David turned out to be the most charming person and we quickly became very fond of him. He was a talented artist and painted a picture each for Wendy and me from the Bambi book which I still have. He would read to us from exciting books and played records of children's stories on his smart little wind up gramophone. I found it was nice to have someone else in the house again. I knew he would not be staying for ever and we were fascinated by the fact that he had girl friends who he used to bring back to the house to meet our parents. They were usually good fun and gave Wendy and me lots of attention.

Eventually David met a girl and became engaged to her. Her name was Sheila and we certainly approved. Wendy and I didn't go to the wedding but our parents did and they moved to a house in Helston and I often used to go and stay with them for weekends in the term time when Wendy was away. Eventually they moved to a small village miles away up country near Callington called Rilla Mill and gradually we lost touch as sadly happens so often in life.

CHAPTER ELEVEN

Growing Up
1959 – 1963

I passed my eleven plus exam in the winter of 1959, much to the relief of my parents as the outdoor life was my consuming interest at age eleven with schooling becoming a bit of a necessary nuisance as far as I was concerned. With Ron gone and Wendy away up country at boarding school I was becoming a bit of a loner and was happiest roaming the cliffs and moors.

My mother took me in to Knights shop in Helston who supplied the uniform for all the local Helston schools. It was exciting to have so many new clothes all at once even if it was school uniform and especially the new pair of more grown up black shoes without laces. As soon as I got home I put on the shoes and walked down to the caravan field to show Nickie who was appropriately impressed. I would be starting school in the September of that year.

So much was changing, people coming and going, our friends Jane and Marianne in the caravan field and Penny and Cherry up the lane leaving for new lives in Canada . It had been a hard slog for their parents to climb back up to a reasonable standard of living after the war years and Canada offered a lot of opportunities at that time. I met Jane and Marianne once more many years later when they returned for a visit but our lives had gone in such different ways that we no longer shared any common ground it seemed. Penny and Cherry I never saw again. Other Henscath school friends of our age moved away up country or abroad or to private schools and so in that particular year I was the only pupil from Henscath to go on to the grammar school in Helston. That summer of 1959 was one of the finest driest summers known for years in Cornwall and with my dear sister home for the summer holidays we made the very best of it, swimming and surfing every day that we could. By the height of summer even the sea became warmer. The guest house was bursting at the seams with guests and Wendy and I moved out of our bedroom and into the infants classroom to free up two more beds.

One of the jobs that Wendy and I were given in the summer was to go down to Auntie Nellie's house to collect sacks of crabs for evening meals. The crabs were alive and as I recall generally much larger than the crabs we see now. The sacks were quite heavy and we had to stop several times on the way back up the cliff path. One day as we sat to catch our breath, one of the crabs escaped from the sack and began sidling away. That was when Wendy came up with the great idea that we could have crab races. We would take two or three crabs out at a time and set them at a starting point being very careful how we held them as the one huge claw is very powerful. Off they would go, usually in all directions as crabs only go sideways. Wendy thought it would give them a little more time before they would be plunged into the boiling water where they let out a terrible scream which we could not bear. Of course it was actually only air escaping as my mother was at pains to explain to us, I really do hope it was.

From a very young age Wendy loved to go to church on a Sunday, she enjoyed the Sunday school classes which I have to confess I found a bit of a bore as a young child and as she got older she liked to go to the morning service or evensong at six o clock. I usually went with her but begrudged having to leave the beach early on a summer day to go home and get changed for the walk up to the village. By the time we reached the village we would fall into step with other parishioners and I would still be grumbling about having to leave the warm sand and sea. The church bells began tolling as we got closer to the church and pushed open the heavy oak door blinking as we entered the dark musty atmosphere, the bells now almost deafening. We sat on the cool pews at the back of the church, a different world from the heat, sea and blue skies. The bells became quiet and the vicar glided in in his long black robes, stood at the pulpit and surveyed his small congregation. Hymn no. 434 he stated and the organ burst into life. Amongst the deep Cornish male voices and high pitched sopranos, there floated two pure young voices singing from the innocence of youth.

We got to know some families who were staying for many weeks of the summer in tents and touring caravans in the caravan field. There were kids our age both boys and girls and with them we had beach barbecues and went on walks, sometimes all the way to Kynance cove. We decided one morning with our caravan field friends, that we would all get up really early and go down to Mullion cove and through the cave for some surfing. When we got down there we found there were some good curling waves but the tide was only just on the turn from going out and usually we didn't swim then because of the currents and possible under tow.

Having made the effort to get up so early, the older ones, including Wendy decided to swim out anyway to catch some reasonable sized waves. Soon the tide was coming in quite fast and the waves got bigger so they didn't have to swim out so far to catch them, but us younger ones couldn't go out very far at all and sat watching and envying their rides. Then the waves started to get really big and only my dare devil sister and one of the boys Robin, decided to push their way out through the closer waves to get a longer ride in from the larger breakers further out. It was soon obvious that they should not have gone, the waves were reaching a great height and curling under too hard for a good body surf on wooden boards. When the waves curl too much you are in danger of being tipped right up and somersaulting down into the shallows under the wave. They were helpless in such strong sea and vainly tried to strike back for shore. Suddenly a huge wave came and picked the pair of them up like leaves tossed in the breeze. We couldn't see them at all for a few moments as the wave surged in towards the beach and then tossed them right up onto the beach as if spitting out apple pips. We were all very scared and rushed up to them. Robin and Wendy were badly winded and we were all very frightened in case they had really injured themselves. Thankfully, although bruised and grazed, they were both all right after a few minutes and counted themselves very lucky both to have survived and not to have been thrown onto the rocks. They had been lucky enough to learn a valuable lesson and never took chances with their respect for the sea again.

There were many interesting people who came to stay at Henscath and that summer a couple arrived who subsequently became great friends with my parents. Michael Wharton, otherwise known as the journalist and author Peter Simple and his wife Kate. They were both writing for the Daily Telegraph at the time, Michael with his witty column much loved over the years by many and Kate with her cookery column. Even on holiday they had to submit work to the Telegraph and spent ages on the phone dictating their latest copy. They tended not to stray too far from Henscath just enjoying relaxing in the garden with their young daughter Jane and when we discovered that we had a mutual love for Monopoly, Michael and I would play the game for hours whilst Kate sought out my Mother for long chats in the kitchen. After that summer Michael and Kate would often come to stay as friends

after the summer season and we would
have raucous games of Pit in the evenings
next to a roaring fire.

That last summer before starting at the
Grammar school was one of the happiest I
can remember, but all good things come
to an end and September 1959 came with
the day I should catch the bus into Helston
for the first time full of anxiety and
excitement.

The green Western National double decker
bus swung around just a few feet away
from the edge of the cliff and came to a
shuddering halt outside the Cove hotel
where I dutifully waited with my mother in
my new winter school uniform, new
satchel, new PE bag and shiny new black
shoes. My smart beret meanwhile sat
squarely on top of my head. It would only
be a matter of weeks before it was pinned
to the back of my head to look the least
conspicuous along with the hitching up of
my skirt in the way of my peers but for
now the uniform was slightly too big and
my navy pleated skirt hung further below
my knees than it should have done.

I waved my slightly anxious looking
mother goodbye and climbed up to the top
deck.

It was a ten mile journey to Helston and
by the time we had got half way, the bus
was practically full of 'Green school kids',

their nickname deriving from the emerald green uniform they wore, who were headed for the secondary modern school in Helston and 'Grammar Sows' which was our nickname, though I was never sure why.   I think it was something to do with sower bugs which was the name woodlice went by in Cornwall.

I only recognised a few of the children, although I didn't know them by name as they had been to different Primary schools from me and I began to feel more nervous as they all chatted amongst themselves only giving me a few sideways looks. I quickly realised that I was the only one on the bus who did not have a Cornish accent and instinct told me that it would matter. I was right because the minute I opened my mouth to speak, I got laughed at and some of them mimicked me, repeating everything I said in a posh voice.

By the time we reached Helston I felt thoroughly humiliated. Fortunately I had no problem dropping into a Cornish accent. I loved accents and I had lived in Cornwall for all of my life up to then, so by the time we walked through the school gates until I got off the bus again in the afternoon, I became a proper Cornish girl and was totally accepted by my peers.

Having dropped the Secondary Modern children off at the top of the town, the bus made its final stop outside Helston railway station where the rest of us piled off it and made the final quarter of a mile walk to the well established grammar school built in the early 1900s and proud to have educated Charles Kingsley. One of the first headmasters was Derwent Coleridge, second son of the poet Samuel Taylor Coleridge. The current Headmaster at the time of my arrival in the school being one Mr. Guise who was to leave under rather cloudy circumstances a few years later. For me there was a mixture of feelings in this new somewhat austere atmosphere. We had to call the female teachers Ma'am and the male teachers Sir and there were severe reprimands if we forgot. There was parquet flooring all over the school and the assembly hall with its high stage at one end and walls covered in wooden framed boards depicting all the head boys and girls going back over a hundred years or so. The teachers all stood on the stage looking down on us each morning in their black gowns and mortar boards as we stood in military lines, boys on one side of the hall, girls on the other. There were notices given by the headmaster followed by a reading from the bible by one of the teachers and a prayer and then Mr. Cleek the music teacher settled himself at the piano and we sang wonderfully vibrant hymns. Mr. Cleek with his thick head of black hair sleeked back with brill cream, played short pieces of classical music while the teachers and Head were getting settled on the stage but one morning he played Exodus which was a piano piece that was in the pop charts. We all thought this was terribly daring and he earned his 'cred' with the whole school for always.

If a pupil had committed some awful misdemeanour, Mr. Guise would survey the hall full of pupils in such a way that we all felt guilty and then he would suggest that whoever was the perpetrator of the crime, should come to his office and take his or her punishment, if not the whole school would be kept in their classrooms for every break time. It always worked and the guilty pupil would have to take his or her punishment. It was the style of his punishments which eventually lead to Mr Guise' dismissal along with the deputy headmistress.

At lunch time we all queued up in the boys cloakroom where there were three hatches opened up revealing the kitchens. Generally the lunch was served from three huge aluminium bowls. One with mashed potato, one with swede or some such vegetable and one with some sort of watery grey stew, all served from a large ladle by the cooks. All very Dickensian

really although I never heard anyone ask
if they could have some more! The food
was pretty awful on the whole, only
cheered up sometimes with a pudding like
spotted dick and lumpy custard.
I didn't like the school at all, it felt a bit
like a prison to me, humourless teachers,
one of whom I remember particularly. Mr
Shimmins, a short bald ancient chap who
always wore his black gown and he carried
a long thin stick at all times . He taught
religious instruction . We had to have our
bibles open at the appropriate page in
front of us and our hands flat down on the
desk either side of it. We were only to
look forwards or at the print in the bible.
Shimmins moved silently up and down
between the desks holding forth on
whichever piece of text we might be
currently reading. If he found himself
next to you and thought that you may
have turned your head for a moment or
moved your hand, down would come the
stick in a whipping action across the back
of your hand while he barked his
chastisement. I dreaded RI and learned
nothing from Mr. Shimmins, the lesson for
me was spent glancing at the watch on my
outstretched wrist and wishing the time
away.
Some of the teachers were lovely of
course. The English teacher Miss Lomas

for instance who also lived in Mullion and who continued to keep my interest in English literature as my father had done before but all in all they appeared a strange bunch and I was very unhappy. At age eleven I was deeply self conscious. I was a little sturdier than most and very aware of it so I became the class clown in order to give a different persona to hide behind. Unfortunately I got so into it that my school work began to suffer as a result and I got into a lot of trouble with the teachers and spent a lot of time being kept in to write out discipline cards. The discipline card was a long and boring description of what discipline meant and depending on how naughty you had been, had to be copied out once or several times and handed in when finished. I reached the point when I could have repeated the words verbatim but thankfully I have now forgotten every word. Looking back of course it was such a shame as I had loved my schooling up till then but now I hated every minute of it. It would be a long time and only just in time that I finally stopped regarding school as some sort of punishment and made just enough effort to get through some GCE's as they were called then.

I made some good friends at Helston Grammar and one day one of them asked if she could come to my house after school and stay to tea. It wasn't until we were actually getting off the bus that I realised there was a problem. At home I was expected to speak with the London accent spoken by my parents whilst at school I had a thick Cornish brogue. I decided that the best thing to do was not speak unless absolutely necessary. My mother noticed that I was being unusually quiet and asked if I was okay. I nodded but when she asked to be introduced to my new friend I knew the game was up. But to my surprise when I opened my mouth to speak, what came out was a most extraordinary mixture of London and Cornish all rolled into one. Somehow I seemed to get away with it from all sides, although not without the odd raised eyebrow from my mother which I knew was a sign that we would be speaking about this later.

I met up with a girl at the Grammar school who was to become a lifelong friend. Kip as she was always known, real name Wendy, lived in the village and started at Grammar school the following year. We travelled on the same bus to Helston and soon found we had the same interests and love of the wild and the animals that belonged to it. We appreciated the country around us and the sea. We were growing up fast and enjoying a bit more freedom. We roamed the moors and cliffs which were in our blood all through the winter and spring and in summer the beach days were numerous. We would visit Jo and Graham up on the cliff in the hopes of being allowed to have a go with their air gun, we took them mushrooms freshly picked on the way to their house just as Wendy and I had done on occasions.

In another year or two we would attend the local dances at the Womens Institute and discover that boys were attractive even if they didn't dance much but just stood in groups trying to look cool, while we danced to the music of local groups playing sixties music. We did the jive and the Twist and hoped the boys would notice us.

We joined the badminton club and walked home in the pitch dark unable to avoid the hundreds of slugs that were all over the pavement when it was damp. Sometimes we would dare to walk over the slugs in bare feet and peel them off when we got home. How gross can the child's mind be? In the summers we swam by day and in the evening there would be huge beach barbecues where we all begged borrowed or pinched food and drink to take down onto the beach where we made a fire from driftwood and listened to the beach boys on a ghetto blaster. Sometimes we would swim in the dark, much more scary than daytime swimming as the imagination went wild as to what might be lurking nearby.

We were only thirteen or fourteen and were so lucky to have had so much freedom. Looking back I see that we were all incredibly naïve, probably because there was so little outside stimulus. The television programmes were all very restricted and it was only when the likes of Cliff Richard and Elvis Presley and later the Beatles and the Stones who we revered, came on the scene that it dawned on us that there was a bit of a different world out there. In the sixties at the height of drug taking and flower power none of us had any contact with drugs at all, the nearest we got was a can or two of Newcastle brown ale and the odd poached cigarette. How lucky for us that the naivety prevailed.

However it may have been a different story. One afternoon I walked to the beach with a couple of boys down from London on holiday. One of them took something from his pocket and offered it to me. He said it would make me feel good. It was a large purple tablet. I wasn't quite sure what it was, it didn't exactly look like a sweet so I declined, some sort of instinct telling me it was a bad idea. I was fourteen at the time and although now it sounds unbelievable I had never heard of drug taking even though it was so prolific.

It would be a very long time before mobile phones and home computers were invented and there were probably more houses in Mullion without any sort of telephone than with one. Life was not so 'urgent', so 'now', you had to learn to be patient and wait for things and as young teenagers we had very little money to spend as there were very few jobs to go round. We made use of the things that were free around us. I earned a little by helping in the summer with the washing up and turning the beds down in the evening and Kip helped her neighbour who took in a few guests although that came to an untimely end when she inadvertently managed to tip a jug of iced water down the back of one of the male guests.

By 1962 the heavy workload at Henscath began to take its toll on my parents and they started talking seriously about the unthinkable – leaving Henscath and moving back up country. With Wendy training for a career in dance, it was unlikely that she would be returning to Cornwall much when she left school and with the dire work opportunities in the area my parents were concerned for me getting into a decent career when my turn came to leave school. There was nothing imminent about moving away but the seeds were being sown and I just prayed it would never happen.

But it did happen, in September 1962 my father went away to Exeter University to do a refresher course and was accepted at a school in Surrey as Head of Economics and in the utterly appalling winter of 1963 he left for Horley in Surrey to stay in lodgings and begin his new career while my mother stayed behind to do a little more teaching and carry on running the guest house for a while whilst packing up the house for the return up country.

There was a house sale and I watched so many familiar things being snapped up. I couldn't quite grasp that this was really happening but it was and I was going to have to accept it very soon.

Wendy at this time was starting out in her first paid dancing job so there was only my mother and me to sort everything out and once again I doubt I was much help. A little of me was excited at the prospect of being near London and a new life in the suburbs but my attachment to Cornwall and Mullion in particular was much greater, I kept thinking something would happen to halt it all.

My father returned to Mullion for school holidays and my mother went up to Surrey a few times to look for a new house with him and in September 1963 my Godparents came down to pick up my mother and me to transport us to our new home and new beginnings in Horley.

We both wept as my Godfather drove us away down the lane, I think for my Mother some tears of relief that the workload was now over but for me tears of sadness, a whole new chapter was about to start and I wasn't ready to finish the old one.

Mullion Cove (Henscath second from right)
before the bungalows were built between Henscath
and the Cove Hotel

CHAPTER TWELVE

The Spell of Cornwall

As with the beginning of my parents lives in Cornwall nearly not happening due to the falling of a bomb in Penzance, their leaving of Cornwall was so nearly marred by a near tragedy. In the winter of 1961 along the Polurrian cliffs on the opposite side from Journeys End where they had spent their honeymoon, there was a house which was in a precarious position as the cliff face was eroding closer and closer to it. Eventually it was declared unsafe and the people living in it were told they must get out over the next few months. They decided to have one last big party before leaving the house to the clutches of nature. My parents were invited to the party along with many other people and by all accounts there was much drinking and dancing, the party finished in the early hours and everyone went home to face their sore heads the next morning no doubt. The owners of the house had barely crept into their beds when they heard an ominous cracking noise followed by an enormous crash of glass, whether or not it was the weight of all those people dancing or that the danger was much greater even than they had been told but they got up to discover that the house was now falling rapidly over the edge. It was lucky that their bedroom was facing the lane and not the sea because the whole of the walls and windows at the back of the house fell in one go. They only just got out in time. Sad enough that they had lost their home but how much sadder it could have been if it had taken all those people with it.

The House that fell over the cliff at Polurrian 1961

I remember once as a small child being asked by a kindly lady on the beach if I was having a lovely holiday. "I'm not on holiday" I told her "I live here" She asked me where I went for my holidays. "I don't go anywhere" I said proudly "I like it here."

It honestly never occurred to me that there might be somewhere else to go to for a holiday. If holiday meant playing on the beach and in the water, then why would I want to go anywhere else? We went up to Plymouth once a year to buy new clothes in Dingles department store where I would go up in the lift and down the escalators over and over again until the lift lady told me off. Plymouth had been bombed extensively in the war and the rebuilding process was still in progress when I saw it as a young child. Seeing the devastation of the bombed sites was scary and hard to understand why. I remember lying in bed in the hotel hoping that it would not be bombed. I loved the wide streets and pavements and looking out to sea from Plymouth Hoe trying to imagine Francis Drake setting off with his fleet to destroy the Spanish Armada. We spent the weekend there in a posh hotel where you could see out of the lift and our treat was to go to the cinema on Saturday night.

It was there that I saw my first Tod-Ao wide screen film, Pat Boone in April Love on a screen so big I could hardly believe it. The following year we saw Ben Hur with Charlton Heston. But after two days in the city I was very pleased to get home to the ever changing world I lived in.

On a fine summer's day you can look down into Mullion harbour and out towards the island and the pale green sea will be as clear as a mirror and you can see down through the water to the sand and rocks. If you are really lucky on such a day you might also see some basking sharks. We didn't worry about the sharks when we were swimming as basking sharks only prey are plankton small fish and fish eggs. Now swimmers have to be a little more cautious as other types of shark are seen. Sometimes the sea is prussian blue, sometimes it turns white with whipped up fury when the harbour is awash and huge waves break over rocks and walls. Occasionally a seal might find its way into the harbour for a while before heading home to its secret cave under the cliffs. Now the secret caves are invaded by coasteerers, wild swimming enthusiasts exploring places we never dared go. The moors are ever changing yellow with gorse bushes or purple with heather and cascades of sea pinks or thrift flow through the vegetation clinging to the side of the cliffs until they practically touch the sea over spring and early summer. In the winter the moors are moody and brown and clouds cast black shadows across them, the odd glimpse of sun sometimes lighting on a pale grey rock covered in yellow lichen. Purple mallow used to cover the Island in Spring, although that no longer seems to happen.

When shafts of sunlight danced on the water in Mount's Bay Wendy said it was God's fingers reaching for the sea. The change was constant, often surprising, never boring.

There is nothing some elderly Cornishmen like more than to weave a story to an unsuspecting holidaymaker in the pub. Some of which no doubt are partly true. One such elderly chap introduced the element of shock in the Wheel Inn at Cury cross lanes whether by design or not would be difficult to say. He once got the attention of a young woman whose husband was chatting to the barman. He leaned towards her. "I've had terrible trouble with me old arse today" he confided. The lady looked uncomfortable and glanced to her husband for support but he was still deep in conversation. "Yes" he continued "I've ad trouble with 'in fer months, sometimes e goes alright but sometimes don't matter 'ow 'ard I push, nothin 'appens. But today was worst of all I squeezed meself round the back and pushed fer all I was worth. Don't mind telling ee I were exhausted by the time ee popped out"

This in the fifties was pretty shocking stuff but the lady ever remembering her manners managed a watery smile and tried to walk away.

As she got up the old man said "Would you like to come outside and see me old arse?" The lady flew to her husband's side and told him what the old man had been saying. He marched over to the old man and demanded he apologise to his wife.

"What fer" said the old man "it's true, you come and see" He rose from his bar stool and the husband followed him out into the car park where a beautiful chestnut mare was standing tied to a post. "This is me 'arse " he said.

There were many stories concerning people who had drowned, with the fierce currents and undertows in many coves and bays, it is an unfortunate fact that most summers there are some drownings and people falling from the crumbling cliffs. In Mullion the St John's Ambulance was often called out for people who had ventured too near to the unfenced cliff edges. Stories abound about drowned bodies being found standing up in the sand after being washed up on the beach and in the fifties and sixties there was a small reward given to anyone who found a dead body on the beach. In my youth there was a story going around the village about a man who had fallen from his fishing boat and drowned. When he was pulled from the water they discovered that one of his feet had been severed. He was a local man and the village gravedigger Charlie duly dug his grave in the churchyard where the man was buried some days later. It was a few weeks later that a local boy found the man's foot still in its boot washed up on the beach. He took it to Charlie assuming that he would open up the grave to bury the foot with its unfortunate owner.

It was some time later that Charlie, well inebriated in the Old Inn one night, recounted the story and told a shocked audience that it was a hot day and he hadn't felt like digging the grave all up again so he had tossed the boot and foot down the end of someone's garden. Another tale to shock an unwary visitor? Who knows?

It is of no surprise that there are so many myths and legends in Cornwall, from the brooding, unchanging Bodmin moor with its dark pools, scattered rocks and craggy hills appearing through thick mists like giant sentinels, to the wild, windswept cliffs of Lands End and Lizard Head.

On the approach to Mullion cove there is a turning onto a steeply descending road which after a quarter of a mile rises steeply on the other side as it leads up to Predannack where there is a leper graveyard and many ghost stories surrounding an ancient Celtic cross. I remember as a very small child, attending the crowning of the Cornish Druid Bard there.

The descending part of the road has always been known as ghost hill and whether you believe in such things or not, many people have had an odd chill in their spine there. On a very rare visit by my grandparents once, they passed the top of the hill knowing nothing about its reputation and my Grandfather gave an involuntary shiver and said "Ooh ghosties and ghoulies down there"

It is said that in the beautiful Bochym Manor halfway between Mullion and Helston, there is a patch of blood on one of the stairs after a duel many many years ago, which if cleaned away, will always reappear. Bochym lies in a valley with its own microclimate where plants seem to flourish particularly well including enormous gunnera plants. Although picturesque, the place certainly does have a certain inexplicably spiritual feeling about it.

The Old Inn in the village is also said to have a friendly lady ghost who appears in one of the bedrooms from time to time.

I had an experience which began when I was a small child at Henscath. Personally I am not a believer in ghosts and I don't think that what I experienced could be attributed to such, nevertheless it was a very odd happening and occurred on many occasions.

I have previously mentioned the very long corridors in Henscath with the kitchen being at one end of the house and the lounge at the other. When I was about four years old, the family were in the kitchen one early evening when my mother asked me to go to the lounge to fetch her packet of cigarettes and lighter. Only the lounge hall between the corridors was lit, making the corridors just light enough and shadowy. The end of the corridor outside the lounge had been cordoned off to make a small telephone room and house my mother's treadle sewing machine. I skipped happily down the corridors and into the lounge to pick up the cigarettes and lighter but as I came out of the lounge I felt a very strong feeling of fear and that I must run for my life. As I started up the corridor I heard the telephone room door burst open and out from the corner of my eye I could see a giant behind me in huge boots. I could hear the treadle on the sewing machine going backwards and forwards. The giant began to catch me up and lunge over me but I ran just fast enough to get to the dark lobby before the kitchen door where immediately the giant disappeared. This was all totally real to me so you can imagine how terrifying it must have been. Why I didn't burst into the kitchen and tell my parents, I really don't know , I just composed myself and walked back in as if nothing had happened. After that I was prepared to risk any sort of telling off when I refused to go on an errand in the evening which involved going to the other end of the house but sometimes I just had to go, forcing myself to take the steps forward towards the lounge and past the telephone room where the whole scenario would repeat itself. I came to realise that the treadle was being worked by a giantess, probably his wife and she was waiting for him to bring me back so she could chop my head off.

There were a couple of occasions when I had a very similar experience at the Blue

Peter Club in the village which also had long corridors. The experience went on for two or three years after that.

Although now it all seems ridiculous and the vivid imaginings of a child, I still remember the extreme fear and the realness of it. The only reason I have to question it is because I am now an adult with rational.

Tin mining chimneys stand eerily all over Cornwall as a constant reminder of days gone by when Cornwall had its own working identity before the boom of the tourist industry. Gweever, Poldark Wendron, Wheal Jane to name but a few and the last mine to close was South Crofty mine in 1998 after a brave fight to keep it open despite depressed world wide tin prices. Cornwall's tin and copper miners were so skilful they were called for all over the world and many left for distant shores and a good wage. But many came back to Cornwall eventually, unable or unwilling to break their ties with the county. A community of Cornish mining families grew up in the extreme south west of Ireland which has many similarities to the Cornish coastline and they remain there still, the future generations growing up as Irish. It was a hard life and many a miner lost his life in treacherous conditions. Many a ghostly story evolved from the mining communities. The mine at Wheal Coates goes all the way down to the sea. You can hear the sea crashing if you listen through the grating in the floor of the ruined Towanroath engine house, a famous industrial building. At low tide it is possible to access the mine shaft through a large cave on Chapel Porth beach. It is said that the mine is haunted by the ghosts of the many miners who died there from working in such hazardous conditions.

Places such as St Just and Camborne and Redruth which were the capitals of Cornish mining, literally became ghost towns as the mines closed around them but the Cornishman will never be put down and these towns are now thriving again with such as the holiday industry.

The ghost stories are numerous from howling dogs to moaning voices and grey spectres seen roaming the moorlands and story telling is in the blood of the Cornishman.

Jamaica Inn, built in the mid 1700s and immortalised in Daphne Du Maurier's book of the same name, is reputed to be one of the most haunted places in England. Of the many ghosts seen there, the only menacing one is a highwayman in a three cornered hat walking through doors and is frequently seen. It is said that a distressed young mother and her crying baby have also taken up residence there in one particular room.

Bodmin jail is also high on the list of most haunted in Great Britain. The jail, now a tourist attraction, still sends shivers down the spine when walking its historic creepy corridors. Selina Wedge, executed in 1878 for the murder of her son, is often seen especially by children as she reaches out to them. They ask why the crying lady in the long dress is so sad.

Dozmary Pool in a particularly bleak and windswept part of Bodmin moor, is said to harbour King Arthur's sword and the ghost of Jan Tregeagle a harsh magistrate who lived in the early 17th century who can still be heard howling across the moors.

Charlotte Dymond, a nineteen year old farm maid was found on the moors near Roughtor with her throat slit. Her crippled lover was caught and hanged although he always protested his innocence. Charlotte's ghost has been seen at Roughtor wearing a gown and bonnet.

The large panther like cat known as the Beast of Bodmin Moor is still seen regularly and given to the savaging of livestock at night. Accounts of the beast teeter between reality and the paranormal.

Locals told of a ghostly Druid seen near Rillaton Barrow offering those he met to drink from his golden cup. When the barrow was excavated in the early 1800's a two thousand year old skeleton was found with a gold beaker by his side. So the ghoulish stories still abound and probably always will. There are many strong Cornish traditional songs and many are about the strength of the Cornish resolve. In 1807 when Napolean Bonaparte was making threats that would affect trade in Cornwall at the time of the invasion of Poland, the following song evolved:-

'Come all ye jolly Tinner boys and listen to me
I'll tell ee of a storie shall make ye for to see
Consarning Boney Peartie, the schaames which he had made
To stop our tin and copper mines, and all our pilchard traade
He summonsed forty thousand men, to Poland they did go,
And for to rob and plunder there, you very well do knawa
But ten-thou-sand were killed and laade dead in blood and goare,
And thirty thousand ranned away, and I cante tell where, I'm sure.
And should that Boney Peartie have forty

thousand still
To make into an army to work his wicked will,
And try for to invade us, if he doesn't quickly fly-
Why forty thousand Cornish boys shall knawa the reason why.'

The Cornish heart beat seems to have the strength to always overcome. With the loss of its great industries it has always found a way to survive and so much of it is due to the place itself and the Cornish people; it will always be worth the fight.

Printed in Great Britain
by Amazon

19550559R00144